FINDING BUDDHIST PATHS IN 21ST CENTURY

Dealing and Overcoming Worldly Distractions

Tashi Gelek

EDITED BY David Gration

BALBOA.PRESS
A DIVISION OF HAY HOUSE

Balboa Press books may be ordered through booksellers or by contacting:

Balboa Press
A Division of Hay House
1663 Liberty Drive
Bloomington, IN 47403
www.balboapress.com
844-682-1282

Print information available on the last page.

ISBN: 978-1-9822-7072-8 (sc)
ISBN: 978-1-9822-7074-2 (hc)
ISBN: 978-1-9822-7073-5 (e)

Library of Congress Control Number: 2021912872

Balboa Press rev. date: 08/16/2021

May my journey offers helpful insights

from the words of the Buddha

to curious Buddhist path-seekers and even some non-Buddhists

I dedicate all the merits to those who are under the influence of

worldly distractions

I dedicate this book to my late Father Tashi Phuntsok, late Mother Kunchog Tso, wife Yangchen, and son Tsering.

Contents

Foreword

This book is to help Buddhist believers incorporate more Buddhist practice—and more effectively—into their lives, using realistic Methods to find their path.

I hope you will gain as much learning, satisfaction, and fulfillment in *reading Finding Buddhist Paths in the 21st Century* as I have in editing it.

From my experience working with Tashi Gelek in the years of the journey so far to his Buddhist path, this note aims to help you to gain more from your study of this book. Attempting to be an objective outsider to some extent, I can tell you impressive things about Gelek, which he is too modest, in his consistent Buddhist Humility, to write. I can be more assertive to present his credentials and successes. In this way, I hope to build your confidence to learn through him, here from the very start.

Gelek has much to offer us from how he has combined his family life and responsibilities with path-seeking and into path-dwelling, strengthening both loving family cohesion and Buddhist practice in the process. Similarly, he has integrated his demanding time-consuming work responsibilities, under considerable pressure, with his Buddhist practice. He is a senior international manager for a major multinational company, and his Buddhism — far from drawing his energies away - has further enhanced his work effort and efficiency to the benefit of the company. I confirm from my knowledge and observation that path, family, and job are all better from this synergy,

The elements of your life might be similar or different, but the Methods Gelek will set out are for adaptation to seek your unique paths. The guidance is all very practical, and there is no need for conflict around Distractions. Family, Work and Path are not competing for limited time and attention and do not have to give way. As Gelek writes in his Preface, "there is no need to disband our lifestyles."

This note is not about editing, a dull subject which can be boring with some other books. It is only a means to an end, and here the end is the journey to the personal path. I have witnessed but also hope - to use his word - *shared* - Gelek's journey. For me, this started when I was the academic supervisor for his successful doctorate and Thesis about Compassion and Guanxi in managing and dealing with Chinese enterprises. We continued through close association and family friendship towards editing.

The most significant contribution in this Foreword is as observer and reporter of a tangibly effective relationship between Buddhist practice and the rest of life. In our context, between path, family, and work, Buddhism obviously predominates for this book and Gelek. Of the three, it is the one where I am least competent by far. I know much more about homes and families and business management jobs and careers.

For this reason, my supporting role is subsidiary. The entire credit for this book is Gelek's alone.

This book and the journey it describes follow the sequence Learn, then Seek the path, to dwell in the path. Now you can learn here, then seek, and dwell in your own found Paths.

It might surprise you that your editor for this book is not a Buddhist.

When Gelek invited me to edit, he obviously knew this, and the gulf between us in terms of knowledge of the book's subject did not perturb him. He saw that this could be conducive to editorial objectivity. A non-Buddhist editor could question statements which a devout Buddhist, already convinced, might skip over as the familiar truth. No suggestion they are not, but there might be a benefit in clarifying apparent inconsistency. On the other hand, the non-Buddhist would have less knowledge of derivation and context. But the only impediment to my editorial objectivity is friendship with Gelek, and I hope to have successfully demonstrated that the friendliest way to help an author is to be objective. This has not been difficult as I do not deal with the spiritual but practical application to life.

It was clearly for Gelek to explain Buddhism. What could I add to the spiritual heart of the book? My job was to edit, but how much I have learned about life from this privileged introduction to Buddhism. More than Gelek has learned about writing from my editing: he was already a naturally accomplished writer.

I explained to Gelek that not only am I not a Buddhist, but I am also an atheist. The author was still not put off and saw this as adding further interest and a dynamic boost to the mix. I hope his confidence is not displaced and that you, dear readers, will not be offended and will be intrigued by the paradox.

So this remarkable man set out calmly to write a book about Buddhism edited by an atheist.

I am not an atheist with a capital A, I am not active, committed, organized, signed up, nothing collective. Only atheistically inclined, casually. It is not something I have thought about very much, not thought it through as Gelek has, deeply, his Buddhism. I am simply not a religious person, religion has never been part of my life, but I am not opposed to religion. Nobody has the right to be that. I respect and admire your religion. Without envy?

But it's remarkable, all the same, this Buddhism-atheism aspect. I suppose the one similarity is that we both think we are right, but the Buddhist, more convincingly, has more guidance, sources and will have thought it through more deeply, certainly comparing Gelek and me.

There is a great deal to learn from *Finding Buddhist Paths in 21st Century*:

- You are probably a knowledgeable Buddhist believer on the way to seeking your Path. Tashi Gelek has you in his sights and wants to help you intensify active Buddhist practice in your life. You are open to exploring the book's practical Methods, willing to choose those combinations which suit your life and wishes. You are in the top priority readership. Your intentions are good, and the book will guide you to convert intention, perhaps vague, into firm realistic plans and clear action.
- You maybe a more general reader, not a Buddhist, of another religion or none. You are interested in spiritual aspects of life and could be, but do not have to be amenable to changes in the way you lead your life, probably less demanding than a Buddhist path. This book does not aim to convert you to Buddhism, which you are probably not thinking of—no more than your editor who says he is too old anyway.
- The book's top concern is the first, Buddhist, group, but the readership has broadened to include the minority second group. I quite like this idea, being in that category myself. Gelek's clear straight writing gives us some idea of

Buddhism (I'm not sure he needs an editor at all) and he has taken further steps to help the non-Buddhist reader. But we must not dilute the benefits for the Buddhist potential path-seeker.

• An example of this balance is a modest experiment with Information Panels which explain some basics with which Buddhists are already familiar. The Buddhist reader can skip these and move ahead without being distracted or bored. We have not overused the device. Part of my job has been to help non-Buddhist readers

I would now like to summarise chronologically the aspects of Gelek's journey which I experienced.

Professor of Management, after many years in real international business management, I was designated in charge of Gelek's doctorate. His scholarship was impressive, with sound scientific research methods and his talent for thesis writing. Also, the clarity of thinking, direction, and analysis, along with well-planned and intelligent hard work. I was equally struck by his devout Buddhist beliefs and practice.

Unlike Gelek's, my PhD Theses have little relevance for Buddhist paths in the 21st century. The 1st was an immature and procedurally routine anthropological study of the Masai tribes in East Africa sixty years ago, with nothing useful for 21st century Buddhism. The 2nd was a study of organisations in Moscow during the 1980s for the All Union Institute of Systems Studies but again with nothing we can use here.

Regarding my research expertise, I applied my training in research methods to industry throughout my managerial career, as well as but less, academically. Management is not a Science in the sense of laws and principles from empirical research. It is short of those, but it is a Science (and in the light of the previous sentence has to be) in applying Scientific Method to managerial situations. All managers, not necessarily consciously, do research because, without much guiding theory, every management situation is an experiment to be systematically explored and learnt from. The same will apply to your experimental search for your path.

In every job in each company, industry, or other organisation I worked for and with, in addition to researching my methods, I properly constructed wider research projects which each successfully achieved a positive result, to reduce staff turnover, to increase the proportion of women at each level of management, to reduce external recruitment and increase internal promotion, to improve negotiating skills and success from comparing methods of successful and unsuccessful negotiations—giving a few examples. The purpose of research should always include making the world in some way a better place. I had effectively applied these methods in projects with Xerox, Standard Chartered Bank, Gallaher (Benson and Hedges), CERN, Digital, Chloride, and many other companies as a consultant. Good consultancy should always be research.

I would most of all draw your attention here, however, for your own journey, to Gelek's sense of organizing different actions and priorities and the quality of disciplined commitment and time management. I was observing Gelek at the start of his path seeking, already fitting together his learning and practice of Buddhism with family responsibilities and relaxation as loving husband and father, and at the same time with all his business responsibilities and big complicated strategic decisions. All while putting in the time, effort and concentration to complete a rigorous full doctoral program with its substantial research and writing demands. His work, particularly in Buddhist countries, fed into his research and his Thesis added knowledge, skills and ideas for his job and commercial success. There were no losers - wins all round.

Following the doctorate, I was fortunate to stay in touch, and came to know better Gelek's delightful close family and home and saw how this was the centre of his Buddhist strength and the source of his business energy and motivation. We became friends, and I enjoyed their hospitality. The warm feeling as I stepped into their house taking off my shoes, sensing the friendship and faith, and anticipating Yanchen's cooking delicious momo. I continue to enjoy all this in between periods of COVID confinement.

We discussed at length Gelek's fascinating job. Already familiar with the high-powered international business environment from my career, I discovered further Gelek's work around the world and the problems to be solved, including in Asia's different Buddhist countries and cultures, many of which we both knew and exchanged stories from. We knew and respected, for example, Japanese culture and management methods. I didn't know much about Buddhism, but I did about Confucian Compassion.

It was not all serious, and we had fun wandering around Zürich's old town and cafés with sunny memorable boat trips on the lake. It was all memorable.

I had been honoured, flattered, and intrigued when Gelek invited me to edit his new book. Along with the first, Buddhist-atheist paradox came another remarkable difference between us. It was about Death and life after death.

I am grateful to have learnt about Guanxi from the Thesis, and more recently, amongst many other discoveries, about Samsāra and Śūnyatā, which has clarified much in my own life. I am, was, a Social Anthropologist, and my field is not so much the differences between cultures which can lead to conflict, but the similarities, what we have in common and can build on for cooperation. Remarkably similar but different practices, rituals and artifacts exist in other geographical regions, different cultures and races. Also, different socio-technical systems, industries and types of organisations—educational, medical, religious, business, tribal, sporting, military get up to the same sort of things. And centuries and more apart: similarities across space and also across time.

Guanxi exists in various forms under different names around the world and so does Samsāra — Śūnyatā. However, the Buddhist and Compassionate cultures are exceptional.

But - I am unable to come to grips with life after death.

The first Chapter draft Gelek gave me to read was Chapter 4: Death. I was gripped by the whole Buddhist approach to death, quite apart from life after it. I have been absorbed into the magnificence of Living Consciously—Dying Consciously, having been previously preoccupied only with the first half of the concept. This is very clear to me and of tremendous importance. I do not repeat the details that Gelek has explained so carefully but do please study through the whole step-by-step process. Read about *The Tibetan Book of the Dead*, and read how *Death is Great Teacher*. Consider deeply each *Bardo* in each of the *Bardo* Types. Apply each step that means most to you and which fits your life.

Another feature of my part in this experience is that Chapter 4 has enabled me to come to terms with my death, up to its physical point. And another aspect of death is its imminence. I am 84 this year and have a severe cardio-vascular-cerebral condition. There is consequently a very high probability that I am closer to death than the much younger Gelek, apparently in good health. Another intriguing difference in our ways of looking at things perhaps.

With the help of Chapter 4, I have been able to limit my talent for prevarication—i.e. able to face up to things—and have settled problems and consequences for and between the many branches of my large and dispersed extended family. Without Chapter 4, I was sweeping issues under the carpet, left to sort themselves out afterwards.

I am now able through Chapter 4 to make the most of my remaining time, to be more considerate, and to repair some damage from earlier mistakes.

In the top level of vulnerability due to age and health, I am one of the first to have been double-dose vaccinated properly—due to chapter 4! I have misgivings about these first vaccines. It is astonishing how little we know about what real protection they are likely to give. The sales patter from big pharma businesses, and the desperate ramblings of politicians seeking undeserved popularity and votes, have left too many unanswered questions. I would like to hear more from medical science and less from amateurs. But Chapter 4 got me thinking less selfishly and more about other people, especially those I love. Never mind my opinions, and never mind about my life after death. What about their life after my death? I realised that my many children, grandchildren and great-grandchildren were worried that the old man was refusing to be herded into vaccination. Gelek also. So I am vaccinated.

If I have been mistaken about life after death—and I can see that it is more subtle, and feasible, than I had previously bothered to consider—then there is one thing of which I am sure, and it is this: I can see very clearly Tashi Phuntsok and Kunchog Tso extremely proud of their son Tashi Gelek as they follow and guide his Path.

I have been writing this Foreword as a "satisfied reader," benefitting greatly, rather than as editor. If I single out one "highlight" for me, it is the subject of Death but only in the context of all the others. Your greatest gain may well be a different topic. I am only an example. The book is all examples to encourage you to find your own path. From my experience, you can be optimistic, and certainly from Gelek's.

One example is a feature of Pluralism, in the sense that whatever divides us, we can find something else we agree on, and build on that. Overlapping interest is not possible in a non-pluralistic relationship or society (South Africa under apartheid; Northern Ireland during "The Troubles" with separated Catholic and Protestant at war).

In addition to religion or the lack of it, author and editor differ in other ways: generation, culture, politics, tastes, computing, and other skills. These do not matter, make relations more interesting and need not turn into conflict, especially if we ignore them. More important and useful are the things which unite us and are the bases for productive collaboration: philosophies of management, appreciation of Compassion, motivation. We agree broadly about Money and Success, Habits, other Distractions, Shift, most ingredients from the book. We have compatible approaches to time, planning and organisation, co-operation. We both think we are humanitarian, peaceful, tolerant, and so on, pretty good sorts all round in our terms. Rightly or wrongly, but we can work together productively and have done so.

We each have multicultural commercial management success under our belts and, in addition, academic interests and work. My career moved from anthropology to business to education as separate stages. Gelek combines Buddhism, executive work, and staff training all together, at which I marvel. Atheism has not taken much of my time.

To conclude, Education. Gelek and I both teach, but he is reluctant to call himself a "teacher"—Humility—and this a teaching book. We are wary of didactic instruction, but helping people's learning is what counts. Exchanging experiences is an excellent learning-teaching method, of which *Seeking Buddhist Paths in 21st Century* is a fine example.

Gelek has not waited to until his arrival to publish his journey, which would be impressive but not so helpful, perhaps daunting for the rest of us. By reporting in progress, we are all learning together. Book and sources take us through the Buddhism learning stage, guiding your choices of methods and practice to your *decision*—by the end of the book?—to become a path seeker. You can't seek until you have decided that you are now a seeker. You can't do anything until you have decided, inside yourself, that that is what you have now started to do—not while dithering.

I wish you every success to that point and beyond, Path Dweller. Thank you for reading this Foreword if you didn't skip it. Now for the more interesting reading.

David Gration
Switzerland
March 2021

Preface

The malicious and contagious Coronavirus (COVID-19) spread across the world from Wuhan in China like wildfire. The virus attacked all nations. The pandemic has changed our world in unimaginable ways: visible sufferings and hidden blessings. On the one hand, the anguish from deaths, economic losses, and helplessness; on the other, disguised blessings from togetherness, quality-family-time, reorganization of work, and egolessness.

All of the nations experienced thousands of deaths and millions of sufferings. Many went through prolonged lockdowns bringing their economies to a standstill spiking unemployment rates, and exasperating economic suffering from income loss. All of us felt helpless. The intelligent human race was not able to control the menace of the virus. This small virus almost brought the entire world to its knees. As ordinary as we are, we panicked and searched for solutions and methods to overcome it. Suddenly at the mercy of our mother nature. And it continues.

It shows how vulnerable and weak we are, vividly expressing the impermanent nature of our existence by consuming so many lives so rapidly. The notion that death can come to anybody and anytime is cruelly exemplified. The deaths resonate with the teachings of impermanence by Buddha Śākyamuni—as relevant now as it was 2,500 years ago.

On the other hand, there were subtle blessings around us during this crisis. The sufferings helped us to open our arms of togetherness and hugged us with love and compassion. People were forced, due to lockdown, to spend more quality time with their parents, husbands or wives, children, partners, pets, or themselves. We could share more stories, incidents, events, problems, and jokes—taking us back into the memory lanes and cherishing the sweet memories of alive and dead. The fear of infection and the inability to find a cure reduced the huge egos we have. Self-fulfillment is replacing self-chastising. Peaceful and quiet dinners with your loved ones instead of chasing after appointments.

The deaths and sufferings around us sparked an idea of sharing my fifty years journey of Buddhist path-seeking and path-dwelling. I want to share my trials and tribulations and some success as a path-seeker, various distractions during my life so far, effective methods to overcome challenges in the path, and other useful approaches for ordinary people like me.

My wife Yangchen confirmed the significance of sharing the story. We had many candid and open discussions about relating the experiences to maximize the benefits to others, resulting in the genesis of this story of my journey, to help in an extremely practical way.

Many believe that practicing Buddhism is more for monks than for laypeople. But my evolutionary journey in the Buddhist path shows otherwise—another compelling reason for writing this book. I will show how an ordinary layperson can migrate from a path-seeker to a path-dweller. Great news! The possibility of mingling practice with daily worldly lives offers opportunities to husbands, wives, business people, entrepreneurs, gays, lesbians, married, singles, and so on. There is no need to disband our lifestyles.

Like any ordinary 21st century busy-life-style individuals, I went through a multitude and different layers of societal hurdles and personal family hindrance in starting my practice. I feel great joy in having started the journey. My path-seeking is interwoven inside the experiences of different types of distractions in life and connections with Buddhism. Incorporated in these personal stories are the relevant Buddhist teachings that have profoundly influenced my path-seeking journey. I also share what I have learned about Buddhist teachings and other non-Buddhist bonus benefits in life. The simplicity of the journey and reflective nature of the stories will relate to those of you who face similar challenges in life in different shapes and forms. We are all the victims of distractions, in the Buddhist sense. None of us can evade this until we achieve complete liberation. And liberation is the ultimate goal of a Buddhist path.

This is an experience and best practice sharing book with referential case studies, not a Buddhist manual for seeking a correct path. For guidebooks, people can read readily available books on the teachings of Lord Buddha in English and easily accessible information on the internet. For teaching, there are many qualified Buddhist masters. I have acquired the understanding of Buddhist sūtras through hearing and reading, contemplating, and practicing from my mind. My understanding is far from complete. The selection of a suitable path is the decision from your analysis and choice. But I hope readers will find some connection to my experiential journey to enable them to start a Buddhist path and find new ways and opportunities to practice, in becoming more aware of how to overcome worldly distractions.

The 84,000 teachings of the Buddha Śākyamuni are manifestations of all the different paths available for individual capacities and aptitudes and circumstances. The biographies of the past Tibetan masters teach us not to give up on seeking wisdom in this lifetime. May your reading of this book offer a new direction to pursue a Buddhist path, to seek a genuine master, to put words into practice, to become a genuine practitioner, and to attain a more profound realization of the wisdom during your life.

Chapter 1

Blessings

Remembering your teacher is
the entrance-way for blessings,
ultimate method for realization of wisdom.[1]

The phenomenon of "Distraction" is a vast subject in Buddhism. We can even state that the essence of Buddhism is to conquer— too strong a word, more gently overcome—our distractions. Our distractions can take on different forms, and a concise definition is that all that takes us away from the truth is a distraction. The theme of distractions is an integral part of this book and interwoven throughout its chapters.

Distractions are core reasons that prevent us from embarking on a path of Buddhist practice. The distractions as disguised in different forms have the power to keep you attracted and attached to them for many years unless you intentionally try to free yourself.

I am writing about distractions because, in my past life, I am not alone in having been distracted from practicing Buddha Dharma for worldly reasons—some from necessity, many from

---

[1] Great Patrul Rinpoche. Padmakara Translation Group, 1998, p. 309.

habit. We are attracted to distractions because they are so potent. The combination of potency and our habits produces a perfect recipe for distraction.

Only at forty-three had I gathered sufficient courage to start a Buddhist path nine years ago in 2012. In the earlier years, I was busy with all sorts of distractions that kept me away from practicing Buddhism, though I was born and raised in a Tibetan Buddhist family. In this book, I will take you through my journey of getting lost in the labyrinth of distractions and finding a suitable Buddhist path. Also, I will share my understanding of Buddhism, personal experiences, observations, and advice from the great masters of the past and the present. And I hope and pray that you will find something valuable and motivating to start your seeking.

In the following chapters, I have addressed different types of distractions that I face during my life as:

- Chapter 1: First Distraction Future Dreams.
- Chapter 2: Second Distraction Money and Success.
- Chapter 3: Third Distraction Habits.
- Chapter 4: Fourth Distraction Death.
- Chapter 5: Fifth Distraction Family Attachment.

My Buddhist Family

I was born in a Tibetan family in which both my parents—father Tashi Phuntsok (1924-2016) and mother Kunchog Tso (1935-2017)— were practicing Tantrayāna (Vajrayāna) Buddhism of the oldest

Nyingmapa school.[2] Consequently and naturally, like many other Tibetans, I was exposed to the Vajrayāna path from my childhood.

It is too early to discuss Vajrayāna because it might be rather abrupt for some from other Buddhist traditions and non-Buddhists to comprehend its methods. Many Tibetan masters have said that Vajrayāna is a path that is swift but volatile at times because it uses every potentially available method—as ignorance, anger, pride, desire, and jealousy—to realize the wisdom. This apparent paradox will become clear as you read more information in later chapters. For example, there will be more information about using emotions as methods in Vajrayāna to discover wisdom. One must be prepared thoroughly before embarking on this challenging journey under the guidance of a genuine tantric master. This advice should be considered seriously, or you will face many obstacles along the path.

This background profoundly influences my writing. And, I don't intend to conceal my exposure to and belief in Vajrayāna.

I don't aim to write an academic book, but it will include many valuable references from multiple teachings from Sūtras (Skt.) and Śāstras (Skt.).[3]

My knowledge of Buddhism comes from studying the words of the Buddha and the commentaries by renowned Buddhist masters of the past and present. Also, I have included some of my testimonies

---

[2] Tantrayāna Buddhism is studied and practiced predominately in Tibet, Bhutan, and other Himalayan regions, but now slowly spreading in other parts of the world. It is also known as Vajrayāna or Vajra Vehicle or Secret Mantra Vehicle. It lies at the heart of the Mahayāna Buddhist tradition. Based on the motivation for achieving awakening of oneself for the benefits of others, this path is centered on developing pure perception. It contains skillful methods for accumulating merit and wisdom to swiftly and directly realise the Buddha nature. The skillful methods include visualisation, deities worship, mantra recitations, and meditation.

[3] The sūtras are the words spoken by the Buddha, and the śāstras are the commentaries of the teachings of Buddha.

of the ongoing Buddhist spiritual journey and the words that I have heard from my late father. Honestly, I am a path-seeker in the beginning stages of the voyage. Everything in this book is what my mind can and has comprehended so far.

Without further ado, it is essential to discuss some fundamentals of Buddhism.

In the film Matrix, there are two types of pills: blue and red pills.[4] The blue pill means that nothing changes, and life returns to normality. But the red pill shows the true nature of Matrix and the way out of the bondage from it.

In the Buddhist context and my interpretations, the blue pill represents samsāra (Skt.), and the red pill the truth about the samsāra. The distractions around us lure most of the people to choose the blue pills. Fewer opt to select the red pills. Most of us don't want to be liberated from this samsāra due to attachments to our parents, siblings, husbands, wives, children, grandchildren, careers, adventure, exploration, friendship, love, and so on. We love our tangible and real world. Everything new to us can be hard to realize or imagine.

Visualizing the illusory nature of our world seems to be much harder to imagine than holding the branch of a tree. The śūnyatā (Skt.)[5] or emptiness nature of the forest is almost impossible to conceptualize when thousands of trees stand in front of your eyes. We are still struggling to understand the emptiness of existence,

---

[4] Matrix is interesting from a Buddhist perspective. It uses modern communication methods to show the bondage of a matrix world (samsāra) and liberation from the slavery (truth).

[5] Śūnyatā means emptiness in Buddhism. It is one of the main teachings of Lord Buddha in the Prajna Paramita Sūtra, also known as The Heart Sūtra.

although Buddha Śākyamuni taught the wisdom in the Prajna Paramita Sūtra 2,500 years ago.[6]

The book uses the "Information Panel" to help non-Buddhist readers to comprehend Buddhist concepts and general topics.

Samsāra and Śūnyatā

Figure 1. Buddha Śākyamuni inside the Mahabodhi Temple in Bodh Gaya, India.

---

[6] The sutras faithfully recorded the words of Lord Buddha.

> ### *Information Panel 1*
>
> • *Samsāra: It is the "tangible" and comfortably familiar and apparently "real" world, "normal" life, nothing changes.*
> • *Śūnyatā: It is the truth that liberates us from bondage, habit, and ultimately from samsāra.*
> • *Why would we choose samsāra over śūnyatā? We don't want to leave our attachment to family culture and members, love, and friendships as we fear adventure and exploration. Or, we might like the idea of leaving samsāra but can't as the notion of śūnyatā and liberation is harder to grasp and act on— even if we do want to give it a try—because of our habit of attachment to our world.*

The Journey of Distractions

I have faced many internal conflicts during my journey of practicing Buddhism. In this book, I will explain all the different types of distractions during the various stages of my life so far.

On a profound level, distraction is any of the emotional responses we are sidetracked by, for example, hope for praise, fear of blame, lost in thought.[7] In Buddhism, distraction is the mother of all emotions. All emotions are broadly categorized into hope and fear.

I have made clear that my primary motivation for writing is to benefit people who intend to pursue a Buddhist path. To give some hope of the possibility to practice in a hectic lifestyle, for all others who are nervous about seeking or are distracted in other ways to practice.

These are my personal and subjective opinions. If these

---

[7] Dzongsar Jamyang Khyentse, 2012, p. 29.

experiences are helpful, apply them in your lives; or read the book as personal testimonies of an ordinary person.

Thinking all this through as a writer has strengthened my resolve to overcome distractions and laziness, and committing publicly with a book has added further reinforcement. We often need other people for reference, for example about simply wearing a suit and tie. I might ask my wife whether the color of my shirt matches my tie. I feel more confident about my choice after receiving confirmation, or even acknowledgment from looking in the mirror.

I hope that my unexceptional life experiences as a Buddhist path-seeker could reflect your situation and provide a little more optimism for pursuing your future path. As seekers, we aim to achieve a positive result at the end of the journey. The real possibility to end our sufferings as confirmed by Buddha Śākyamuni.[8]

The Four Truths

The Lord Buddha had spoken the four truths (also known as the four seals or views or wisdom): (1) all compounded (anything made up of constituent parts) things are impermanent, (2) all emotions are pain, (3) all things have no inherent existence, and (4) nirvāṇa (Skt.) is beyond conception.[9]

I will take generosity (Skt. dāna) as an example to describe the four truths. In the first seal, we accomplished generosity more easily by seeing our possessions as impermanent so that we can't cling to them forever.[10]

In the second seal, generosity becomes an act of joy when there

---

[8] Buddha Śākyamuni is the Buddha of our time. He is also referred to as the Lord Buddha, and sometimes as the Buddha.

[9] Dzongsar Jamyang Khyentse, 2007, p. 5.

[10] Dzongsar Jamyang Khyentse, 2007, p. 111.

is no pain of miserliness because we have no reasons to cling to our possessions.[11] In the third seal, you can reap all the fun of the experience of generosity when you imagine distributing a billion dollars to strangers on the street in your dream.[12] In the fourth seal, generosity can be measured by the level of attachment one has to what is given and to the self that is giving it—a perfect generosity is an act without any attachment.[13]

Information Panel 2

The Four Truths:
- *All compounded things are impermanent: Everything we experience through our senses, and all external phenomena, are not going to remain permanent. They have a beginning and an end. For example, a flower will bloom and fall. A person is born and will die. A feeling of joy will arise and end. We are not able to enjoy it forever.*
- *All emotions are pain: All the feelings ultimately lead us to suffer. For example, the birth of a child is a bliss to a parent. But when the same child grows up and gives painful experiences to their parents, happiness turns into anguish.*
- *All things have no inherent existence: All phenomena are empty without an inherent self-identity—for example, a house. When a house is dismantled to its ingredients (cement, rubber, steel, wood, stone, and so on), the concept of the house does not exist any longer. And further disintegration of these components shatters the concept.*

[11] Dzongsar Jamyang Khyentse, 2007, p. 111.
[12] Dzongsar Jamyang Khyentse, 2007, pp. 111-112.
[13] Dzongsar Jamyang Khyentse, 2007, p. 112.Liberation is another term for nirvāna.

> • *Nirvāṇa is beyond concepts: It is the cessation of all the samsaric sufferings. It is a state where you are not bounded by the cause, effect, and result of karma. As a result, one ceases to be reborn and henceforth achieves the ultimate peace.*

The Buddha said that the end of the suffering is achievable at the end of a path. One of the renowned disciples of Buddha, Great Nagarjuna said that the nonexistence of samsāra is nirvāṇa.[14] There are many sights and sounds that can help us realize the truths. For example, when enjoying the beautiful views of changing seasons, remember the impermanent nature of all the beautiful flowers blooming and falling. Japanese celebrate Sakura, cherry blossom season, with great enthusiasm and fanfare because the timing of blossom is unpredictable and lasts for only a short duration.

The compassionate Lord Buddha showed 84,000 different paths for different types of people in the world. It is an à la carte menu with so many choices. Wonderful!

Karmic Link to Buddhism

As a teenager in high school in exile in India, I was not very fond of listening to my parents' guidance about reciting Tibetan Buddhist mantras. We often had novice and lay monks coming to stay with us for long periods reciting mantras and reading from the Buddhist sūtras. It was not the events in the day that excited me but what followed in the evenings.

The most entertaining moments were when they would sit around for dinner and start talking about their past lives in Tibet and commonly known friends and relatives. These Tibetan folk tales

---

[14] Dzongsar Jamyang Khyentse, 2007, p. 106.

were full of fights, love, marriages and often ended in brave banditry episodes. In between their conversations, they cracked a few jokes on my sister and me for being *yeshu*.[15]

In my childhood, playing with balls, sneaking to the Yamuna river, and stealing mangoes were more exciting and fun than going to a *gompa* (Tib., monastery) or sitting in for a *wang*.[16] I always tried to find excuses for not attending such ceremonies. Sitting idle and silently was a harrowing experience. On the contrary, I was fascinated to listen to the exciting stories about Jesus Christ and his miracles.

For ten years in the Christian missionary school, we had Bible classes, and our Ladhaki school's principal and a priest told many stories from the Old and New Testaments during Sunday sermons. I found many stories of Jesus Christ fascinating and exciting but never developed faith and devotion. Although I also remember that the school tried hard to convince us to believe in The Father, Son, and Holy Spirit. During that time, no Tibetan student was converted to Christianity.

Why did I never have any inclination to become a Christian? Because I had a stronger karmic link to Buddhism, not so evident at that time. But now I can see the link when looking back. Let me explain this point with a short story.

Kyabjé Polu Khen Rinpoche (1896-1970)

Kyabjé[17] Polu Khen Rinpoche Dorje (also known as Thupten Kunga Gyaltsen but popularly known as Polu Khen Rinpoche) was the *Tsawai Lama* (root guru) of my father. In Tibetan, *lama* has a deeper meaning

---

[15] Tibetan word for Christian. We were studying in a Christian missionary school in India.

[16] Wang (Tib., Wyl. dbang; Skt. abhiseka) means empowerment.

[17] Kyabjé is a honorific title in Tibetan for the "Lord of Refuge:" It is used for higly realised Buddhist masters.

to it: *la* means one who has unsurpassed enlightened wisdom, and *ma* means having affection, love, and kindness greater than a mother. They had escaped from Tibet together in 1959, and my father spent much time receiving teachings and empowerments from his guru.

Polu Khen Rinpoche was born in the Polu Valley of Derge, Kham in eastern Tibet. He learned to read and write in Polu Monastery and studied with Gönchen Shar Lama Jamyang Chenrap, one of the students of Great Jamgön Mipham Rinpoche.[18] Later he became the abbot of Polu Monastery. He also received profound teachings and empowerments from great masters such as Drubwang Pema Norbu, Jamyang Khyentse Chökyi Lodrö, and Khenpo Ngawang Palzang, his principal teacher.

Figure 2. The *kupar* of Polu Khen Rinpoche belonging to my parents.[19]

---

[18] Jamgön Mipham Rinpoche (1846-1912) is one of greatest Tibetan Buddhist masters and scholars of the twentieth century and considered to be Lord Mañjuśrī in human form. Also known as Mipham Rinpoche.

[19] *Kupar* (Tib.) means a holy image of Buddha, deity, mandala, etc. These are objects of worship for the Tibetans, often venerated and placed inside monasteries and family altars.

At Dokhol Monastery in Trom, Mahasiddha[20] Nyönpa Ngawang Chimé introduced Polu Khen Rinpoche to the nature of mind by merely nodding his head three times.[21] Polu Khen Rinpoche meditated in many prominent power places in the central and southern provinces of Tibet. During one occasion, he met the Compassionate Vimalamitra[22] in the form of an Indian sadhu,[23] who used symbolic gestures to introduce him directly to the true nature of the mind that awoke extraordinary realization in him.[24]

In exile in India, Polu Khen Rinpoche imparted the teachings generously to many Bhutanese, Sikkimese, Nepalis, and Tibetans according to their different circumstances and led many to higher realization. Later he was invited to Bhutan by Her Majesty Ashi Phutsho Choden Wangcuk (1911-2003) and lived at the mountain hermitage of Dechen Chöling. On the plateau of Bumthang, Polu Khen Rinpoche had a clear vision of Gyalwa Longchen Rabjam (popularly known as Omniscient Longchenpa) and received the transmission of the enlightened intent.[25] He continued to turn the wheel of the Dharma (Buddhist teachings) at Tashi Gang and other places throughout Bhutan and benefitted countless beings.

On November 16, 1970, at the age of seventy-four, Polu Khen Rinpoche experienced difficulty breathing—no illness or pain—and

---

[20] Mahasiddha is a tantric master of highest realization accomplished through meditation.

[21] Nyoshul Khenpo Jamyang Dorjé, 2005, p. 531.

[22] Vimalamitra (Skt.; Tib. Drimé Shenyen; Wyl. dri med bshes gnyen) is one of the most learned Indian Buddhist masters who came to Tibet, taught extensively, and composed and translated numerous Sanskrit texts in the ninth century. The quintessence of his teaching is the Vima Nyingtik, one of the heart-essence teachings of the Great Perfection. We believe that he is now residing in the Wutai Mountain in China.

[23] In Hinduism, Sadhu means a religious person who has renounced the world like a yogi. Here it means the outer appearance of a Sadhu.

[24] Nyoshul Khenpo Jamyang Dorjé, 2005, p. 531.

[25] Nyoshul Khenpo Jamyang Dorjé, 2005, p. 531.

told his attendant Kunzang Wangdu that he had no ordinary mind because his awareness had dissolved into utter lucidity and he supposed it to be like what was meant by death.[26] He passed away sitting up straight, his hands palms down on his knees—a gesture known as being at ease in the nature of mind—and gazed into space.[27] His passing had many miraculous signs of earthquakes, the sound of thunder, rainbows, relics of various colors, the skull was not damaged by the flames: inspired awe and faith in his students.[28] His entire life is a truly perfect example of a fully realized *Dzogpa Chenpo*[29] master.

Guru: Misused Word

Nowadays, the word "guru" is loosely used in management, health, fashion, sport, politics, and other fields. It may resemble its meaning in Sanskrit—a teacher or master who transmits knowledge—or it might be casual and insignificant.

In a Buddhist path, one must be guided by a guru. The words guru, lama, master, and teacher are synonyms in Buddhism. The Great Rigdzin Jigmé Lingpa (1730-1798)[30] advised people to do serious research about a guru before trusting them completely.[31]

---

[26] Nyoshul Khenpo Jamyang Dorjé, 2005, pp. 531-532.

[27] Nyoshul Khenpo Jamyang Dorjé, 2005, p. 532.

[28] Nyoshul Khenpo Jamyang Dorjé, 2005, p. 532. The funeral fire consumed the entire body leaving behind the skull. This is considered to be a sign of great realization, often witnessed with renowned masters.

[29] *Dzogpa Chenpo* (Tib.; Wyl. *rdzogs pa chen po*). Refer to Chapter 2 for more detailed explanation about *Dzogpa Chenpo*. It simply means a swift and direct path to realise the primordial nature of mind.

[30] Rigdzin Jigmé Lingpa was a highly realized master and *tertön* (means discoverer of treasure teachings; read more in Chapter 4) of the Nyingma tradition of Tibetan Buddhism.

[31] Dzongsar Jamyang Khyentse, 2012, pp. 85-86.

In Vajrayāna, the guru is the entire spiritual path: the guru is the Buddha, the guru is the Dharma, and the guru is the sangha.[32] A Vajrayāna guru introduces you to your inner guru that is the pure nature of your mind. To reinforce its importance, I have dedicated a section on the Guru Yoga practice in Chapter 5.

There are many stories my father often told me about Polu Khen Rinpoche. Even when I graduated from school or found a good job, or any auspicious event occurred, my father dedicated it to and remembered it as the blessings of his guru.

My father had many spiritual gurus from whom he received precious teachings and empowerments.[33] However, he talked about Polu Khen Rinpoche the most, and I will share some of his anecdotes in this book.

My father told of an incident about an attack by a swarm of bees:

"Once in Mussoorie, when I was about to enter the room, Polu Khen Rinpoche immediately exclaimed that today there was something abnormal about me because he saw a big, black cloud engulfing my whole head. Then Polu Khen Rinpoche asked me to kneel and bend my head. He started hitting my head with both his hands like beating a drum. Usually, when a revered master does such action, Tibetans

---

[32] Dzongsar Jamyang Khyentse, 2016.

[33] The names of my father's teachers: Kyabjé Dudjom Rinpoche, Jikdrel Yeshe Dorje (1904-87, later as Dudjom Rinpoche), Kyabjé Chatral Sangye Dorje Rinpoche (1913-2015, popularly known as Chatral Rinpoche), Kyabjé Drubwang Pema Norbu Rinpoche (1932-2009, popularly known as Penor Rinpoche), Kyabjé Dzongnang Rinpoche, Jampal Lodrö (1931-1987), Kyabjé Dodrupchen Rinpoche, Jigmé Tubten Trinlé Palbar (b.1927, popularly known as Dodrupchen Rinpoche), Kyabjé Dungsey Thinley Norbu Rinpoche (1931-2011, later as Thinley Norbu Rinpoche), Kyabjé Dilgo Khyentse Rinpoche (1910-1991), Kyabjé Minling Trichen Rinpoche, Gyurme Kunzang Wangyal (1931-2008), Kyabjé Dudjom Rinpoche, Sangye Pema Shepa (b. 1990, later as Dudjom Yangsi Rinpoche) and others.

believe that it removes obstacles in life. I thought the same way. After beating for a while, Polu Khen Rinpoche said that now is fine. After the audience, I was walking through a hilly, rough road in the wood. Suddenly, a swarm of big, black wasps started chasing me. Trying to run fast, I fell to the ground, and all the bees started stinging my head. I was overwhelmed. As a result, I passed out. Later I was rescued by a bystander who threw a woolen blanket over my head. Had it not been for the beating of Polu Khen Rinpoche on my head, I would not have survived this ferocious attack. It was the blessings of my guru that saved my life."

Some people might find this as a coincidence, but my father adamantly believed that it was the blessings of his guru. All of us believe in something. Belief is one thing that we humans are good at. It includes all the types of believers in our world: believers of something and believers of nothing.

Blessings of Kyabjé Polu Khen Rinpoche

My mother had many miscarriages before my birth. So my father sent a letter to Polu Khen Rinpoche in Bhutan requesting his blessings. Polu Khen Rinpoche sent a letter to my parents with a boyish name Tashi Gelek. My parents were so delighted and filled with confidence that this future child will survive by master's prayers. After my birth, my younger brother also survived. No more miscarriages. This episode does not imply in any manner that I am a holy person. Instead, I consider this as an auspicious *tendrel* (Tib.) in my life.[34]

My parents followed a traditional Tibetan system of requesting

[34] The Tibetan word *tendrel* means that all phenomena come into existence through a dependent relationship with other phenomena. Usually used for auspicious events.

a realized Lama to name a child. I followed the same tradition for my son Tashi Tsering. I believe that compassionate masters will give names with boundless blessings and prayers; I think that their compassion indeed creates a karmic link to *konchog sum*[35] in this present or future lifetime.

I used to think that the blessing from Polu Khen Rinpoche was the karmic link that ignited the spark within me to pursue the path of Buddha Dharma. This spark arose in 2012, pulling me towards the Buddha Dharma, and since then, my intention to practice the Dharma is becoming stronger. These positive shifts in my life have become the primary motivation for publishing my experiences.

First Distraction: Future Dreams

When I was in primary school, Kyabjé Dzongnang Rinpoche, Jampal Lodrö (1931-1987), had asked my father to put me in the Mindroling Monastery in India. The Rinpoche believed that I would be good at *cham*.[36] Looking back, I would have expected my father to have agreed to Rinpoche's suggestion. But, unexpectedly, he put me into a Christian missionary school—my first miss to practicing a Buddhist path.

My father desired to enroll his two sons in a Tibetan school in Mussoorie, but the school had only one quota per family. Therefore, my younger brother joined the Tibetan school, and I a Christian school.

Sometimes I wonder what would have happened if I had become a monk. Would I have remained a monk for my entire life? Would I have left the monastery? How would my life be as a monk? Would

---

[35] *Konchog sum* (Tib., The Three Jewels) in Buddhism means The Buddha, the Dharma, and the Sangha.

[36] *Cham* is an elaborate spiritual dance in Vajrayāna Buddhism.

I like or dislike it? So many questions emerge when I think about it. There are no easy answers.

Indeed, I would have complained about my status as a monk and always dreamt of leading a life as an ordinary person. Because we are not always satisfied with our status quo—the grass is often greener on the other side of the fence. As always distracted by either our past or future, we seldom live in the present moment. Visualizing and planning future dreams builds a virtual world yet to arrive. Expectations and anticipation make the future appear more spicy and exciting.

As a child, my future was the biggest distraction full of dreams, plans, excitement, entertainment, money, successes, career, and so on.

As a poor Tibetan refugee, I had big dreams but a silent reminder deep inside me of the limitations as a refugee. Reality check. Often, my confidence was marred with skepticism, hope with dejection, success with failure, excitement with malaise. There was no time and room for self-reproach.

From my own experience, I believed that the future of any refugee child is unpredictable. Refugee children around the world are currently going through the same emotions as I did. Our hearts go to those who have perilously crossed the Mediterranean and barely survived, often traumatized—tortured, raped, lost family members on their journey.

Like most Tibetan refugee families, my parents were illiterate and had to struggle to earn minimal household income to sustain our family. From a very young age, I was determined to become an educated person and make a living from my knowledge and professional skills, never to face all the brutalities of life as my parents did. The drive to succeed in life was immense, like a roaring lion.

The determination was positive, but there were limited possibilities if I had to search for sponsorships for my higher education. After graduating from high school in India, I was in the doldrums. Our family had no money to send me to any college, but I was determined to study further.

Success comes to those who dare to dream. Fortunately, I was enrolled in a scholarship program by the Taiwanese Government for Tibetan refugee students in 1989.

During this period, going to Taiwan was considered a defection within our exile-Tibetan-communities in India and Nepal. The 'Taiwan issue' was a complicated and delicate matter. There were baseless allegations that Tibetan students going to Taiwan were inflicting severe damage to Tibet's cause. Anyway, Taiwan's scholarship gave me a ticket to pursue and fulfill my childhood dreams of a college education.

As an impoverished nineteen-year-old refugee boy, I was too intimidated to land in an ultra-modern Taiwan. During this time, Taiwan was one of the fastest-growing economies in the world, with impressions of progress everywhere. At that moment, I strongly felt that I was in the right place at the right time. I am profusely grateful to the Government of Taiwan and its people for offering me and other Tibetan refugee students the opportunity to pursue their dreams of higher education. This was the beginning of my journey in Taiwan, and also the beginning of the second phase of my distraction towards materialistic success.

Chapter 2

Materialism

Form is Emptiness,
Emptiness is Form,
Form is not other than Emptiness,
Emptiness is not other than Form.[37]

This above-quoted mantra from The Pragna Paramita Sūtra might be too abstract, difficult to understand. Even seasoned Buddhist practitioners can comprehend the essence of the emptiness of this mantra only after much study, contemplation, and practice. We see that the word emptiness appears four times in the short mantra. It is a fact that realizing emptiness in this materialistic world is difficult but important. In this chapter, I will explore the meaning of emptiness and its significance in a Buddhist path.

One of the obstacles to understanding the concept of emptiness is the nature of our materialistic world. Taiwan provided the perfect field for planting the seeds of my future worldly dreams—opening doors to many possibilities. After graduating from National Chengchi

---

[37] If non-Buddhist readers are confused, in the later part of the chapter there is a complete separate section about the Pragna Paramita Sūtra which will help better understanding.

University in 1995 with a Business and English degree, I eagerly raced towards many opportunities in Taiwan.

Taiwan and Tibet

Before going into the next Distraction and the rest of this Chapter, let me pause to gauge the similarities of social values and religious rituals between Taiwanese and Tibetans.

From 1989 to 2000, I made many good friends in Taiwan, and most are still in contact. Our friendships have bloomed into family friends. Taiwanese are warm and kind-hearted people. The two societies have many similar traits.

Both cultures have a strong generational heritage of passing beliefs from parents to children. The elders are highly respected in a family. Taking care of the old family members is considered one of the essential responsibilities of the children. Like in Vajrayāna Buddhism of Tibet, there are many gods and goddesses in Taiwan. The popular ones are sea goddess Mazu and Guan Gong, but there are many other local deities. All across Taiwan are dedicated shrines built for these deities. One of the fascinating phenomena I witnessed in Taiwan was about Guanyin.[38] Guanyin is in the male form in Tibetan temples and altars but appears in female form in Taiwan.

Like Tibetans, Taiwanese celebrate their religious events and ceremonies with loud drums, gongs, bells, cymbals, Chinese trombones, and plenty of fireworks. There is a spectacular experience of nine days of Mazu pilgrimage when hundreds of thousands of pilgrims from Taiwan and abroad escort and welcome a palanquin of a statue of Mazu across the island.

---

[38] Guanyin is the Chinese name for Boddhisattva Avalokiteśvara (Skt.; *Chenrezig* in Tibetan; the Buddha of compassion).

Figure 3. Avalokiteśvara (Guanyin; *Chenrezig*) is in the female form at the altar of Zhongshan Market, Taipei.

Unlike Tibet, Taiwan has a democratic political system and a modern economy. And Taiwanese government offers a world-class health care system with universal coverage at nominal costs. As a result, it has created one of the best medical infrastructures in the world. During the COVID-19 epidemic, Taiwan has adopted a proactive response coupled with daily briefings by the medical officials. Consequently, Taiwan has a lower number of infected cases and fatalities, with a population of twenty-four million. By July 4, 2021, it has one of the world's lowest deaths pro-rata to the population.[39]

During the eighties and nineties, Taiwan was at the forefront of the computer revolution producing computer hardware from factories in China for the whole world. In the initial stages of development, Taiwanese entrepreneurs were the earliest investors who established the production facilities and sub-contracting networks in China that propelled China to dominate the global supply chain.

---

[39] Taiwan Centers for Disease Control.

Second Distraction: Money and Success

After graduation from University at twenty-five, followed by the termination of scholarship, I needed a job to sustain my living in Taipei. My dream career was in the thriving computer industry.

During this time, the computer hardware industry boomed in Taiwan with famous companies such as ACER, BENQ, TSMC, UMC, ADI, LITE-ON, and many others. The Taiwanese contract manufacturers were making products for computer giants such as IBM, DELL, HP, COMPAQ, MICROSOFT, INTEL, etc. I was fortunate to work for some of these companies: ADI (in Marketing Communications, which I enjoyed but preferred a sales job) and LITE-ON (this is where I got into sales, traveling to Europe and the USA for key accounts including IBM and ACER). Then to BENQ India as Managing Director India to start their business there, which required me to complete the rapid maturing process which had been developing with the steadily mounting pressure from job to job. I had learned every aspect of big business and how to manage an entire organization.

The salaries in the computer industry were higher than in other sectors, and so were the career opportunities, with discovery, early responsibility, excitement, achievement, personal development, and other non-financial recognition. Money was the "Key Performance Indicator (KPI)" for me.[40] Now I have a completely different perspective on money. At that time, necessity and ambition were the key drivers: the need for sustaining my living and supporting my parents in Nepal and the ambition to achieve success measured by earnings. The combination was the perfect recipe for igniting the desire for material success.

I worked long hours and continued after-work networking and making friends to build guanxi. This means a relationship between

[40] KPI is a term often used in measuring the performance of an employee in a company.

people, in simple terms. Guanxi is very important in the Chinese society of Taiwan. You might be surprised to know that it is as essential as it was in the past, but it has come of age and evolved into different forms to comply with the local government laws and companies' ethical regulations.

Information Panel 3

Guanxi: Guanxi is deeply-rooted in Confucianism and emphasizes the reciprocal human relationship.

A comprehensive definition:[41]
- *The delicate art of building and nurturing a mutually beneficial relationship.*
- *It spans a long period of time.*
- *Based on the four principles of trust (respect and knowledge of others), favor (loyalty and obligation), dependence (harmony and reciprocity, mutual benefit), and adaptation (patience and cultivation).*

There are different types of Guanxi, such as Jia-ren Guanxi (family members), Shou-ren Guanxi (relatives, friends, neighbors, colleagues, classmates), and Sheng-ren Guanxi (acquaintances or strangers).[42]

The practice of Guanxi is relevant even today in different parts of the societies in China, Hong Kong, Macau, Taiwan, South Korea, Singapore, Malaysia, Indonesia, Vietnam, Japan, and other nations. However, it has taken different forms and uses methods that comply with local laws and customs.

---

[41] Tashi Gelek, 2013, p. 291.
[42] Tashi Gelek 2013, p. 292.

After much effort, I had managed to get good jobs in sales and marketing in renowned computer hardware companies. From the beginning of my career until 2000, I was absorbed and distracted by my profession.

Indeed, keeping busy was one of the significant factors distracting from practicing Buddha Dharma. In business, I felt that any relaxation was wasting my valuable time. Time was money. All my time, I was either busy at work or enhancing my guanxi network.

At this juncture in life, I was paying lip service to Buddha Dharma. I lightly promised my parents when they asked me to recite daily mantras. I hardly did any. Yet, I did claim myself to be a Buddhist without thinking and knowing much about Buddhism. This claim was my limited definition of Buddhism. The true essence of a Buddhist path was unknown to me until I read about it during my late forties. Through hearing, reading, and contemplation, I learned about the true meaning of a Buddhist path.

Information Panel 4

Dr. David Gration gives another perspective of how to view Money and Success, which could be called Motivation and Success. He has many successful years of senior practical management experience in major international organizations (Xerox, Standard Chartered Bank, GALLAHER, CERN) and teaching and researching management and motivation in Universities and Business Schools across Europe, England, and the USA:

There are two factors: motivation within the job itself, in the work we do, and what comes to us from outside the job, from the environment within which we do the work.

As a link to the next section of this Chapter—adding more wisdom to a method—let us explore our work motivation through those two factors.

Within-the-job motivators:
- *Interesting work with a positive sense of purpose and clarity of expectation.*
- *Targets for improvements, variety of new and creative projects, sense of direction, challenge.*
- *Delegated responsibility, freedom from supervision, discovery through new projects.*
- *Learning and growth for achievement, training, and development.*
- *Recognition, including even bigger and more motivating jobs.*

From the environmental factors:
- *The physical environment of working conditions.*
- *The security environment around our job: terms of employment.*
- *The social environment at work: if colleagues are hostile and we feel outcast, this is miserable.*
- *The more controversial financial environment: too-low pay de-motivates, too-high pay does not motivate, but to pay a generously reasonable salary, increasing steadily over the years, helps all round.*

A vast amount of research—organizational, psychological, and social—internationally and over many decades, lies behind this approach to motivation. Most important, it tallies with the learning from experience of successful managers interpreting their in-job practice.

When David Gration was putting this into practice, he had not been introduced to Buddhism. Now he sees it in terms of Samsāra (working for the money) and Śūnyatā (fulfillment through work):
* *Samsāra is in the environmental factors, familiar, safe, comfortable, no change, don't have to think hard. Śūnyatā is real motivation.*

Read Appendix C to learn more about Motivation and Success.

Now my views have changed about money and success. I remember my father often saying, "Son, all the people want to be rich, but only a few are successful," he said, "because your past karma determines your present wealth and prosperity. It's important to accumulate more merits in this life." These words of wisdom, as I aged, have helped me to come to a balance of money-success and Buddhist path.

Buddhist Path = Methods + Wisdom

Many people imagine serious Dharma practice to be something for the monks in monasteries. It is something far away and not easy to practice in our daily lives.

Of course, all the Tibetan families worldwide have altars in their homes and make water offerings every morning. On Buddhist festivals and anniversaries, Tibetans offer incense, fruits, flowers, and lamps. Does such an act of offerings make a complete Buddhist path? It is part of it.

I have learned that a Buddhist path comprises two key ingredients: methods and wisdom. Having both of them makes a genuine path. Many of us focus too much on the methods and, at times, lose sight of wisdom. No Buddhist path is complete without method and wisdom.

If a method does not lead to the realization of wisdom, it is not a true Buddhist path.

The Omniscient Longchepa explained that understanding the voidness (emptiness) of all phenomena and realization of the emptiness nature of our mind is the highest Buddhist view. Any Buddhist path should not lose sight of this grand view. The Prajna Paramita is perfect wisdom that incorporates everything, the supreme Buddhist view.

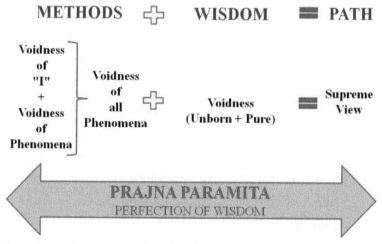

Figure 4. Description of path from "The Four-Themed Precious Garland" by the Omniscient Longchenpa.[43]

To understand wisdom, we have to read the wisdom teachings of Buddha Śākyamuni, The Prajna Paramita Sūtra. It recorded the dialogue between Bodhisattva Avalokiteśvara and Lord Śāriputra[44] while Buddha Śākyamuni rested in a deep Samadhi (meditation). In

---

[43] The book is available for free download at the following website: http://promienie. net/images/Dharma/books/longchenpa_four-themed-precious-garland.pdf. I will not recommend reading it now but when you are ready.

[44] One of the main disciples of Lord Buddha.

the end, the Lord Buddha confirmed what was said about śūnyatā (emptiness), therefore, confirmed its status as a wisdom teaching.

The Prajna Paramita Sūtra

In the Sūtra, the great wisdom of Buddha Dharma is the emptiness nature of everything. Everything includes all our emotions, body and mind, consciousness, and even nirvāṇa. All the realized beings achieved awakening after realizing the wisdom of Prajna Paramita, commonly known as The Heart Sūtra. At a prominent congregation in Rajgir, India, at the Vulture Peak about 2,500 years ago, through the immense blessing of Lord Buddha even while in deep meditation, these words of wisdom were uttered between two of the greatest realized Buddhist masters.[45]

> "Avalokite[ś]vara Bodhisattva
> when practi[s]ing deeply the Prajna Paramita
> perceives that all five skandhas are empty
> and is saved from all suffering and distress.
> [Śā]riputra,
> form does not differ from emptiness,
> emptiness does not differ from form.
> That which is form is emptiness,
> that which is emptiness form.
> The same is true of feelings,
> Perceptions, impulses, consciousness.
> [Śā]riputra,
> All Dharmas are marked with emptiness;
> They do not appear or disappear,
> and not tainted or pure,

[45] Lotsawa House, n.d., *The Sūtra of the Heart of Transcendent Wisdom*.

do not increase or decrease.

Therefore, in emptiness no form, no feelings,

perceptions, impulses, consciousness.

No eyes, no ears, no noise, no tongue, no body, no mind;

no color, no sound, no smell, no taste, no touch,

no object of mind;

no realm of eyes

and so forth until no realm of mind consciousness.

No ignorance and also no extinction of it,

and so forth until no old age and death

and also no extinction of them.

No suffering, no origination,

no stopping, no path, no cognition,

also no attainment with nothing to attain.

The Bodhisattva depends on Pragna Paramita

and the mind is no hindrance;

without any hindrance no fear exists.

Far apart from every perverted view one dwells in Nirv[ā]na.

In the three worlds

all Buddhas depend on Prajna Paramita

and attain Anuttara Samyak Sambodhi.[46]

Therefore know that Prajna Paramita

is the great transcendent mantra,

is the great bright mantra,

is the utmost mantra,

is the supreme mantra

which is able to relieve all suffering

and is true, not false.

So proclaim the Prajna Paramita mantra,

---

[46] Supreme perfect awakening of a Buddha or supreme perfect wisdom.

Proclaim the mantra which says:
gate gate paragate parasamgate bodhi svaha
gate gate paragate parasamgate bodhi svaha
gate gate paragate parasamgate bodhi svaha." [47]

The core message of the Sūtra is condensed in the Prajna Paramita mantra "gate gate paragate parasamgate bodhi svaha": "form does not differ from emptiness, emptiness does not differ from form, that which is form is emptiness, that which is emptiness form." Contrary to common perception, it is not a negation of existence but rather a union of form and emptiness. Realizing this union is most challenging— but achievable—the essence of the wisdom of a Buddhist path. I would recommend you to refer to a realized master to get a clearer understanding and realization of the Prajna Paramita Sūtra.

Those who have received the teachings of the Sūtra should recite daily the mantra as many times as possible. In summary, a true Buddhist path must be based on the wisdom of śūnyatā.

Information Panel 5

The Wisdom of Emptiness (śūnyatā):
- *Lord Buddhas did not create an emptiness. It existed before, during, and after the Prajna Paramita Sūtra.*
- *It is not a negation of existence. Negation would imply that this is something to get rid of. If one clings to emptiness only, one falls into nihilism.*
- *We can have a lot of fun with a Rolls-Royce, but the fun is not truly existing. It is dependent on many causes and conditions. There has to be an individual who is a Rolls-Royce fanatic and*

---

[47] Kwan Um School of Zen, n.d. This is the shorter version of the Sūtra.

has the money and time to enjoy it. The result of these causes and conditions give rise to fun. There will be no existence of fun in the absence of these factors. Therefore, the fun does not exist by itself.

- *There is another ordinary example of a pizza dinner. You need to have some spare time; there has to be a pizzeria; you have money to pay for the dinner; and to be hungry and like pizzas. All these causes and conditions will make up a delicious pizza dinner. There is no delightful taste without these elements. The experience of a delicious pizza does not exist by itself.*

- *Likewise, all phenomena or emotions are the same as a temporary illusion—like a dream.*

- *One cannot realize emptiness through academic analysis—on the contrary, it can only be realized through direct experience.*

When Lord Buddha expounded the teachings of Dharma in India, there arose yet another phenomenon that changed the landscape of the entire Himalayan regions as prophesied by Lord Buddha himself: the arrival of Guru Padmasambhava (Skt.).

Guru Padmasambhava

For most Buddhists, Buddha is the Buddha Śākyamuni. He was the first Buddha of our world, the founder of Buddhism and exemplified the Buddha principle in the Sūtrayāna path.[48] On the other hand, Guru Padmasambhava is the founder of Vajrayāna Buddhism in Tibet and

---

[48] Sūtrayāna (Skt.; Tib. *dö tekpa*) encompasses the teachings of the 'Causal Vehicle.' The path is to establish the cause for attaining liberation through accumulations of wisdom and merit.

therefore known as the second Buddha of our time.[49] He manifested in eight different forms to maximize the benefits to the sentient beings.[50] Historically, he visited Tibet as Guru Padmasambhava, popularly known as Guru Rinpoche (Precious Master) or *Pemajungné* (Tib., Lotus-born) in Tibet and other Himalayan regions.

In the 8th century, Guru Rinpoche was a tantric master from Oddiyāna (current Swat valley in Pakistan), the Nālandā abbot Śāntarakṣita, and Tibet's Great religious king Trisong Detsen established Buddhism in Tibet.

The first monastic University of Samye was also established during this period, which facilitated many Indian Buddhist scholars and Tibetan translators to translate the words of the Buddha from Sanskrit into Tibetan, marking the golden age of Buddhism in Tibet. Due to the merits of the translations, Tibetans have a complete transcription of the Buddha Dharma in Tibetan. Unfortunately, many Sanskrit texts were lost in India.

In Figure 5, the phenomenon of Guru Rinpoche is effective teaching to crush our dualistic thinking. First, the lotus is brilliantly sharp and clean. It grows beautifully in muddy, dirty water and seldom in clean water. Despite its stained surrounding, it can maintain its stainless nature and radiant colors without showing any tinges of dirt. It is encouraging to know that we can keep a flawless nature of wisdom in this polluted world of negative emotions of ignorance, hate, pride, desire, and jealousy. Also, we can be protected from the mighty Maras lurking inside these emotions.[51]

---

[49] Rigpa Shedra, 2019.

[50] Read about "The Eight Manifestations of Guru Rinpoche" in Appendix B.

[51] Mara (Skt. Māra) in Buddhism is the demon who tempted and tried to distract Buddha Śākyamuni from achieving enlightenment. In Vajrayāna, all types of emotions that distract one from practicing Dharma are different forms of Mara.

Figure 5. The *Kupar* of Guru Padmasambhava (Guru Rinpoche) was given to me by my father.

Second, Guru Rinpoche is sitting on the throne of beautiful and fragile lotuses. Based on our dualistic logical thinking and analysis, we are fascinated by the notion of the impossibility of a person sitting on a lotus—something our brains are unable to process. We become the victims of our dualistic minds.

Third, the lotuses are not squashed under the weight of the body, as our common sense tells us they would be. On the contrary, Guru Rinpoche rests comfortably meditating on the lotus throne.

Many Tibetan masters explain that Guru Rinpoche's phenomenon of sitting on a brilliant lotus is already profound teaching to eliminate our dualistic thinking. We are pre-judging lightness and heaviness. Also, our dualistic mind is bogged down by impossibility. Guru Rinpoche is trying to teach us that everything is possible, even liberation from the sufferings of all the sentient beings.

Guru Rinpoche is closely associated with Nepal. He visited this land before going to Tibet. A pilgrimage is like receiving the blessings from Guru Rinpoche through these holy pilgrimage sites in Nepal.

Dzogpa Chenpo or Dzogchen

All the nine perfect vehicles and the Buddha's teachings are the perfections of wisdom that lead to the path of liberation.

The *Dzogpa Chenpo* or Dzogchen practice is the most ancient and direct stream of wisdom within the Buddhist tradition of India and Tibet to realise the true nature of mind.

Dzogpa Chenpo is the Tibetan translation of the Sanskrit word Mahāsandhi or Atiyoga, widely translated as Great Perfection or Great Completeness. *"Dzogpa"* means complete or the end, and *"chenpo"* means great. It is the ground, path, and fruition. The ground is that we are already in a self-perfected state of primordial nature, which requires no perfecting.

Dzogchen has been taught in Tibet through an unbroken stream of highly realized masters until present times. Such great masters as Guru Rinpoche, Khandro Yeshé Tsogyal, King Trisong Detsen, Great Vimalamitra, Great Lotsawa Bairotsana,[52] and others brought and established the unbroken lineages of *Dzogpa Chenpo* in Tibet and other Himalayan regions. It is a perfect and direct practice to realise the primordial wisdom and an effective method during our turbulent times.

Unlike other paths, *Dzogpa Chenpo* provides more profound, swift, and esoteric training to realise the Buddha-essence.[53] The meditation in it is to recognize the intrinsic awareness of the Buddha-essence, and perfection of the realization is the attainment of Buddhahood.[54] The unique distinction is the profundity of its view of the Buddha-essence and the swiftness of its path.[55]

Through the practice of *Dzogpa Chenpo*, in the noble land of India and Tibet, countless practitioners attained perfect enlightenment, and hundreds of thousands achieved the rainbow body.[56]

The rainbow body is not only achieved by monks but also by ordinary laypeople. One such example happened in Yidlhung valley of Kham in Eastern Tibet in 1952. When a Tibetan layman Sodnam Namgyal, a hunter turned devoted *Dzogpa Chenpo* practitioner, died at seventy-nine, he attained a rainbow body leaving behind only

---

[52] Berotsana (Tib.; Wyl. *bai ro tsa na*). The greatest of all Tibetan translators. Lotsawa means translator in Tibetan.

[53] Longchen Rabjan, 2002, p. 92.

[54] Longchen Rabjam, 2002, p. 92.

[55] Longchen Rabjan, 2002, p. 95.

[56] Drubwang Penor Rinpoche, 2017, p. 78. Rainbow body (Tib. *ja lü*; Wyl. *'ja' lus*) a phenomenon of enlightenment is realised in *Dzogpa Chenpo* whereby a highly realised practitioner is able to transform his or her physical body into radiant light.

twenty nails of the fingers and toes along with some hair.[57] There are still many reported cases of rainbow bodies still happening inside Tibet even today. In essence, if you don't realize the meaning of *Dzogpa Chenpo*, you won't attain enlightenment.[58]

It is predicted, in this degenerate time, the *Dzogpa Chenpo* teachings will flourish because it is easy to purify obscurations and attain realization through its practice.[59]

Pilgrimage as the Lighthouse

While working in Taiwan in the nineties, the only moments I thought about Buddha Dharma more seriously was when I visited my parents in Nepal, at least once every year for a few weeks.

They always guided me to all the pilgrimage sites in Nepal and took me to receive blessings from Kyabjé Chatral Rinpoche. On many occasions, they gently persuaded me to accumulate merits (Skt. punya)[60] through circumambulations of Boudhanath Stupa, lighting butter lamps, hoisting prayer flags, and offering *tsoks*.[61]

A person collects great merit by offering *tsok* to a master. On one occasion, I offered money as an offering to Chatral Rinpoche during a *Losar*.[62] Chatral Rinpoche said to my father that he could

---

[57] Longchen Rabjam, 2002, pp. 138-139.

[58] Drubwang Penor Rinpoche, 2017, p. 77.

[59] Drubwang Penor Rinpoche, 2017, p. 79.

[60] Punya (Skt.) means accumulating good karma through good deeds, thoughts, and actions that brings a person closer to the wisdom.

[61] *Tsok* (Tib.; Wyl. tshog; Skt. ganacakra) is a ritual in which a person offers Buddhist texts, Buddha statues, cloths, flowers, foods, drinks, and precious gems to Gurus or Buddhas or deities for their blessings. It is one of the important practices in Vajrayāna.

[62] Tibetan New Year. Lo means year, and sar, new.

use the money to celebrate *Losar* for his *gompa* in *Yangleshö*.[63] My father said, "You have accumulated great merits by making Rinpoche happy during the auspicious time of Tibetan New Year:"

I think the practice of pilgrimage lighting our way to the path is also an effective method of keeping the light of Dharma alive. For many overseas Tibetans, it offers a perfect combination of family reunion and Buddhist practice. I would encourage them to keep this tradition alive by bringing their foreign-born children to the holy Buddhist sites in India and Nepal.

The holy sites of Bodh Gaya and *Yangleshö* are the perfect examples to show the ultimate goal of a Buddhist path as liberation from sufferings. Freedom is achievable as Buddha Śākyamuni and Guru Rinpoche manifested in these holy sites. Not heresy but rather a living proof of its possibility.

I would like to show you some moments of our family pilgrimage to India and Nepal from April 21 to May 2, 2015. It was essential to bring our Swiss-born son Tsering along and let him get familiar with our pilgrimage heritage. At the holy sites, we transferred our knowledge from our parents to Tsering, hoping that one day he will carry forward this practice to his next generation.

At Bodh Gaya, the blessings of the Buddhas are still so powerful and abundant that even non-Buddhists will find peace and harmony within themselves, and the desire to remain in that state irresistible. To Buddhists, it is the holiest site to receive blessings from the Buddha.

---

[63] *Yangleshö* (Tib.; Wyl. *yang le shod*) is called Pharping in Nepali. For Vajrayāna practitioners, one of the holy pilgrimage sites in Nepal. It is the place where second Buddha Guru Padmasambhava attained the state of complete realisation. The place is also closely associated with a wisdom Ḍākinī (simply means a realised master in female form; more explanation in Chapter 4) Vajrayoginī (Skt.; dorje naljorma, Tib).

Figure 6. Yangchen offered flowers in the Mahabodhi Temple in Bodh Gaya, Bihar, the site where Lord Buddha realized the supreme awakening.

Figure 7. Yangchen is teaching Tsering how to make an offering to Lord Buddha inside the Mahabodhi Temple.

At Sarnath and the Vulture Peak, Lord Buddha gave precious teachings of different paths to liberate sentient beings. At the Vulture Peak in Rajgir, India, one of the most remarkable dialogues between Arhat Śāriputra and Bodhisattva Avalokiteśvara about the true nature of mind took place. This event happened out of the blessings and compassion of Lord Buddha. The most precious, profound, ultimate wisdom teaching about Śūnyatā was expounded and witnessed by thousands of Buddhist masters, kings and queens, Gandharvas, laypeople, Asuras, ghosts, and other non-human beings.[64]

Figure 8. Our family offering prayers at the Vulture Peak in Rajgir, India. The Prajnaparamita was taught at this hilltop.

In Nepal, Tsering was able to build a friendly and close relationship with his grandparents. My father was kind to share with Tsering his knowledge of the pilgrimage sites in Nepal. The meeting between

---

[64] In Buddhism, we believe that there are many kinds of non-human beings which are normally invisible to our naked eyes. Only a few realized masters are able to see them.

generations was beneficial to Tsering to understand our Buddhist heritage and culture.

Figure 9. Tsering was playing with his grandfather during a pilgrimage in Nepal. These were the privileged and happy moments between them. Tsering playfully put his hat on grandfather's head in back-to-front style.

I used the occasion to explain and show to Tsering how important it is for him to know about our Buddhist culture and history. My father shared many short stories about Buddhism, which Tsering listened to with interest and asked many questions. These valuable and unique moments of togetherness have left unforgettable memories with us. We hope that one day in the future, this karmic trail will lead Tsering to a Buddhist path.

The pilgrimage to Nepal is incomplete without visiting the magnificent Boudhanath[65] in Kathmandu valley. This great stupa

---

[65] Boudhanath is the largest stupa in Nepal. It is called Khasti by Newars (a tribe in Nepal) or Boudhanath by Nepalis, and *Jarung Khashor* (Tib; Wyl. *bya rung kha shor*) by Tibetans.

has a deep connection with the spread of Buddhism in Tibet. At this site, precious prayers were offered for the propagation of Buddhism in Tibet.[66] Henceforth, at the stupa, it is believed that all the sincere prayers are rewarded if done with absolute faith and devotion. I know many whose prayers have been answered, including my own.

When visiting these holy pilgrimage sites, one should visualize that the past Buddhas had walked and blessed these sites and that whoever visits them will create the necessary condition for a karmic link with the Dharma.

For people living in Europe, America, or elsewhere in the world, pilgrimage can be an exciting journey to Nepal, India, Bhutan or Tibet, offering a unique experience to witness different way of life and philosophies. The chaos in some countries can take a physical toll on you, but if you can find some meaning in how things are as they are could also lead to a journey of enlightenment. Besides the spiritual ingredient, pilgrimage helps me to realize how privileged we are in Switzerland, so I grumble less, and I become more satisfied with my life. It helps to develop a stronger desire to help less privileged societies and people.

In another aspect, it is moving to walk on the same ground as the Buddhas of the past, sparking a light of motivation and diligence to embark on a Buddhist path. Personally, these blessed moments

---

[66] Historically, a local Tamang (a tribe in Nepal) poultry woman called Samvari ((Chadzima (Tib. meaning a poultry woman; Wyl. bya rdzima). Tibetans often call her Ma Chadzima meaning Mother Chadzima.). She built Boudhanath to enshrine the relics of the Buddha Kashhyapa but passed away before finishing it. Later her four sons completed the stupa and made the following aspiration prayers: the oldest brother aspired to be a Dharma King (reborn as the Tibetan King Trisong Detsen), the second brother aspired to be a preceptor of monks (reborn as the Great Master Śāntarakṣita), the third brother aspired to be a powerful tantric yogi (reborn as Guru Rinpoche), and the last brother aspired to be a minister to coordinate the religious activities (reborn as Nanam Dorje Dudjom). They established Buddhism in Tibet.

were conducive for me to contemplate more seriously the meaning of Dharma. But the powerful clutches of my career sucked me back into the realm of business and money until my next pilgrimage.

Figure 10. The photo of Boudhanath Stupa was taken on July 2, 2013 during a pilgrimage.

I would not have imagined that even in ultra-modern Japan, there is a living tradition of pilgrimage called Shikoku Henro.[67]

Shikoku Henro

I have been visiting different parts of Japan over the past two decades. It always impresses and never fails to surprise me. I am humbled by every experience to discover something new about its culture, people, landscape, and religion. We know so many facts about Japan

---

[67] Henro is the Japanese word for pilgrimage.

without really understanding it. All data and no knowledge, no sense of the elusive reality. Japan has also perfected the art of concealing many minute, delicate secrets of their thousand years of culture, traditions, and religion. Writing about all these findings would take a long time, perhaps something for the future.

The large Japanese cities—Tokyo, Yokohama, Osaka, Nagoya, Sapporo—gave the impression that the root of Buddhism is almost invisible. But in a few culturally rich cities like Kyoto and Nara, I felt that the image of Buddhism has survived merely as a past culture and tradition: offering their respect to the Buddhist temples rather than true Buddhist practice. Although I am filled with joys when witnessing Japanese offering incense and candles at holy sites. However, in some selected parts of Japan, I discovered a living tradition of Henro, and one such pilgrimage route is called Shikoku Henro in the Shikoku Island.

In October 2018, I was fortunate to experience a small section of the eighty-eight temples Shikoku pilgrimage route around the island. The great Japanese Saint Ku-kai (Kōbō Daishi), the founder of the Shingon school of Japanese Buddhism, trained and spent time in these eighty-eight temples during the 9th century. Since then, the route connecting all these temples has turned into a pilgrimage route of 1,200 kilometers.

The Shikoku Pilgrimage route has become popular among Japanese but also foreign visitors. People make this pilgrimage for a multitude of purposes: some come for religious reasons, some to pray for healing or safety at home, some for their deceased loved ones, some to get away from their regular life, some for recreation, some to spend time alone in reflection, and some come to discover themselves.[68]

---

[68] Tourism Shikoku, 2020.

Figure 11. One of the temples in the route was hidden inside the mountains.

You can purchase a booklet from any temple, with the names of all the eighty-eight temples. The objective is to keep a record of visited temples: a handy guidebook for completing the pilgrimage over several trips. The temple reception will stamp the page and write artistic calligraphy. This final step concludes your pilgrimage to this temple.

Witnessing the living culture of Sukoku Henro in the 21st century shows that the roots of Buddha Dharma in Japan are still alive in some parts of Japan. I think that this is the blessing of Saint Kōbō Daishi and the collective efforts of the entire Sukoku Island communities. Its existence proves that the light of Dharma is still shining. Through

Figure 12. Left: A booklet to keep track of temples visited.
Right: Stamp and calligraphy to confirm your visit to a temple.

the practice of pilgrimage, the Japanese are making a connection to the Buddha knowingly or unknowingly by sowing karmic seeds that will bear fruits in this life or future lives.

I pray to the Three Jewels that the Henro may continue to flourish across Japan. May Buddha Dharma bloom again in The Land Of The Rising Sun like thousand years ago.

Information Panel 6

Dr. David Gration describes his understanding of the relationship between Japanese management philosophy and Buddhism. His international management experience included working with Japanese management styles, and academic research going into this deeply. It was some time ago and the management context has changed, but the style continues with adaptations because it is deeply rooted in lasting Japanese culture:

The Buddhist foundation for Japanese management "style" and behaviour in organizations not only guides and strengthens management but also enables the path-seeker to secure more time and overcome obstacles to practice Buddhism—which is the aim of this book.

Here are the Japanese management practices which have stayed with me most impressively:

- *Consensus decision process: This takes time, to build the commitment to the better decisions which result from participation, and to defuse potential resistance and power struggles. But it saves more time because consensus decisions are implemented faster and more effectively. This relates to Buddhist patience and generosity.*

- *Teamworking and group working: Organisational harmony in a holistic society goes with a collective rather than individualistic culture. Individuals are not singled out for their performance, which is not distinguished from that of the whole team. This relates to Buddhist modesty, humility, and generosity.*

- *Secure employment: Reinforcing corporate social responsibility, belonging to your organization more than to your specialism or profession means that you are not a production engineer but a Toyota production engineer. This relates to Buddhist diligence and discipline.*

- *Seniority: Steadily upward careers are geared to length of service, with less of the competitive seeking for rapid personal promotions, which can disrupt organizational security. This relates to Buddhist patience and humility.*

The survival of Shikoku Henro is a testimony to the survival of Japanese management style in years to come.

Read Appendix C to learn more about Japanese management.

In this Chapter, we compared the similarities between Taiwanese and Tibetan cultures, looked at the Distraction 2 of money and success, studied the right meaning of a Buddhist path, contemplated on the quintessence of the Prajna Paramita Sūtra, amazed at the phenomenon of Guru Padmasambhava, realized pilgrimage as an effective method of Buddhist practice, and explored the living tradition of Shikoku Henro in Japan.

The ultimate goal of all Buddhist paths is that they are designed to create shifts in our distracted minds to practice the teachings of the Buddha. Despite all the surrounding distractions, I managed to experience a shift that changed the entire perspective of my existence to be developed in the next Chapter.

Chapter 3

Shift

On the one hand, what we call Dharma is very difficult,
but on the other hand, it's very easy
because it really depends on our own minds.[69]

We face many significant challenges in taming our minds. Over the years, I have often heard my Buddhist Tibetan friends and relatives sharing a common difficulty in combining Buddhist practice in their daily lives.

People face many obstructive situations consuming a lot of their time and leaving little time to practice the Dharma. Instead of focusing on studying, training, and gaining experience, many wastes their time on political networking for selfish objectives. Instead of buying a small size living place, people opt for mortgages for big and fancy houses. Instead of raising children happily, parents push them in education in the direction they want them to go. Also, there are so many other distractions that can hold back a shift towards Buddhist practice, as we are prey in the powerful fangs of distractive habits.

---

[69] Dudjom Rinpoche, 1979.

Third Distraction: Habits

The distractions can become habitual patterns. They solidify over some time. We amass plenty of them in our lives—if we let them infiltrate and establish themselves freely, many habits remain forever, some die, and a few weaken.

It took me some time to replace trivial habits with new ones. After a busy three years of my career in India, I moved to settle in Switzerland and start a new family. Then I realized many Asian habits made it harder to adjust to the new environment.

In Taiwan and India, I seldom cooked at home. I always ate outside. In Taipei, the food culture is rich and abundant at reasonable prices. Taipei streets provide many choices. The night markets offer a wide variety of snacks.[70] The ubiquitous twenty-four hours convenience stores remove the necessity to stack up drinks and snacks in fridges. Even at midnight, there are many people in these stores.

But Switzerland is different. There are no twenty-four hours convenience stores or night markets; therefore, people buy household items once for the whole week. Eating outside is not cheap; so, cooking at home is frequent—a small cultural shock. There are plenty of other such differences.

Trivial, but it took me five years to adjust to the Swiss lifestyle. Eleven years in Taipei had solidified the habits that I had to put an effort to adapt. However, Switzerland offers a high living standard, good air quality, clean drinking water, stringent food safety standards, attractive salary, and a properly functioning social security net.

As time passes by, the habits of Taiwan are weakening and

---

[70] A night market is shopping streets full of different varieties of stores and food stalls from late evening until midnight. It is an important part of Taiwanese culture.

49

gradually being replaced by newly acquired Swiss habits, becoming more assertive and dominant.

In hindsight, moving to Switzerland was the best thing that could happen to me. It took more than seventeen years to comprehend its significance to my spiritual journey fully. The serene and less-hectic lifestyle provided the perfect causes and conditions to contemplate pursuing a Buddhist path. It would not have been possible for me in Taiwan—although many genuine Buddhist practitioners live there.

The causes and conditions during the Doctorate Thesis research and the blessings of my master created the shift towards a path-seeking journey.

Beginning of a Shift

My Doctorate Thesis in 2011 about combining business practice and Buddhist compassion changed my life forever. For the research, I read the classic Buddhist texts such as *The Way of the Bodhisattva* by Mahāyāna Indian Master Śāntideva (Skt.; 8th century)[71] and its commentary *The Heart of Compassion* by Kyabjé Dilgo Khyentse Rinpoche.[72] And *The Words of My Perfect Teacher* [73] by highly realised Tibetan master Dza Patrul Rinpoche (1808-1887).[74] The uniqueness of this spiritual guide is its colloquial writing style of describing and explaining complicated Buddhist concepts in simple

---

[71] Śāntideva was one of the greatest Mahāyāna Indian masters. Mahāyāna is the Great Vehicle in Buddhism.

[72] Kyabjé Dilgo Khyentse Rinpoche was one of the greatest Tibetan Buddhist masters in the 20th century.

[73] The Tibetan title of the book is *Kunsang La-Mai Zha-Lung*. Patrul Rinpoche received these teachings from his master Kyabjé Jigme Gyalwai Nyugu, who in turn received it from Ridgzin Jigmé Lingpa. Rigdzin Jigmé Lingpa received these teachings directly from Omniscient Longchenpa through a series of visions.

[74] Dza Patrul Rinpoche (Wyl. *rdza dpal sprul rin po che*) was one of the renowned Tibetan masters of his time. He is commonly known as Patrul Rinpoche.

and easy-to-understand language and examples—although you might need some knowledge about Tibet and Tibetan Tantrayāna Buddhism.

The most significant return on my investment in the research was the beginning of a shift. I became conscious of the things happening around me and started to investigate the meaning of life, a subtle shift-not so dramatic. But it continued, lingering, seemingly to remind me of something. I did not know what that was.

Gradually I started to develop a desire to take refuge in a master. I believe the blessings from the spiritual books triggered the shift. I am convinced that these great Buddhist masters and Bodhisattvas[75] have prayed and blessed their writings to create a karmic link to a Buddhist path for whoever reads them.

Taking refuge is a serious matter. Patrul Rinpoche shows how a Buddhist student should look for a master, what qualities and qualifications are needed in a master, and how to keep the master-disciple Samaya.[76] It is essential to seek a genuine and compassionate realised master. Now I was determined to take refuge in the greatest living *Dzogpa Chenpo* master of our times Fourth Kyabjé Dodrupchen Rinpoche, Jigmé Tubten Trinlé Palbar (popularly known as Dodrupchen Rinpoche). I remembered my father said, "You should find a Longchen Nyingtik[77] guru," "The Nyingtik practice is one of the direct and powerful teachings," he

---

[75] Bodhisattva is a sublime being who vows to help all sentient beings to achieve enlightenment, and sacrifice one's own nirvana for others.

[76] Samaya (Skt.; Tib. *damtsik*; Wyl. *dam tshig*) is secret and holy vows between a master and disciples in Vajrayāna Buddhism. As a good resource about master and disciple relationship in Vajrayāna, you can refer to the speech by Dzongsar Jamyang Khyentse (2018a) "Vajrayāna Buddhism in the Modern World" in Berlin in 2018.

[77] Longchen Nyingtik (Tib.; Wyl. *klong chen snying thig*) is the heart-essence teachings of the Great Perfection. It was revealed by Great Rigdzin Jigmé Lingpa as mind treasure teaching. Refer to Chapter 4 to learn about treasure teachings.

often reminded me as if trying to imprint this message in my mind forever—and he succeeded.

Dodrupchen Lineage

The unbroken lineage of Dodrupchen incarnations has served as the protector and promulgator of the Great Rigdzing Jigmé Lingpa and Longchen Nyingtik teachings.

Rigdzing Jigmé Lingpa is an important master in the Nyingma tradition of Tibetan Buddhism. This itinerant yogi is considered the incarnation of both the renowed Dzogchen master Vimalamitra and Dharma King Trisong Detsen. He experienced visions of many Dzongchen masters (Guru Rinpoche, Khandro Yeshé Tsogyal, Omniscient Longchenpa, and others), wisdom dākinīs, and Dharma protectors. Through these visions, blessings of past masters and long retreats in Tibet, Rigdzing Jigmé Lingpa started discovering *termas*. One such significant and popular mind *terma* is the Longchen Nyingtik teaching.

At twenty-eight, in the evening of the twenty-fifth day of the tenth month of the Fire Ox year of 1757, Rigdzing Jigmé Lingpa went to bed with unbearable devotion to Guru Rinpoche and unceasing words of prayers.[78] While absorbed in the depth of meditative experience of clear luminosity and experiencing flying a long distance riding a white lion and reaching the Boudhanath Stupa in Nepal, Rigdzing Jigmé Lingpa met with a wisdom dākinī who gave him a beautiful wooden casket containing five rolls of yellow scrolls with seven crystal beads.[79] Encouraged by Dharma protector Rahula and another dākinī, Rigdzing Jigmé Lingpa swallowed all the yellow scrolls and the crystal beads, and instantly and amazingly, all the

---

[78] Tulku Thondup, 2002, p. 122.
[79] Tulku Thondup, 2002, p. 123.

words and meaning of the Longchen Nyingtik cycle were awakened in his mind as if they were imprinted there.[80] He discovered the *terma* concealed by Guru Rinpoche in the 8th century to be known as the Longchen Nyingtik cycle of teachings and became a highly realized, revered, and accomplished *tertön*.

The first Dodrupchen, Jigmé Trinlé Özer (1745-1821), was prophesied to be the heart son of the Rigdzin Jigmé Lingpa, who empowered him as Nyingtik custodian, and he received valuable teachings.[81] He was born in the upper Do valley of Nguldza Zalmo Gang in eastern Tibet. Jigmé Trinlé Özer achieved great realization that he could make inanimate objects leap into the air by focusing on them; that he could tame ghosts and reanimate corpses; that he caused a spring to burst forth from a cave in a cliff; that he became the spiritual adviser and teacher of the Kingdom of Derge; and that many from eastern Tibet, China, and Mongolia came to study with him.[82] He revealed many precious *termas*[83] of outer, inner, and secret practices for Buddha Amitābha through numerous visions of Amitābha, and the blessings from Guru Rinpoche, the Omniscient Longchenpa, the Great Rigdzin Jigmé Lingpa, and Milarepa Zhepa Dorje.[84]

In 1821, at the time of the death of the first Dodrupchen Rinpoche, one of his chief disciples, Do Khyentse Yeshey Dorje (1800-1866), was away from his teacher at a distance of a few weeks' travel by horse and wasn't directly informed, maybe for months.[85] But on the day when Jigmé Trinlé Özer died, Do Khytense received a pure vision

---

[80] Tulku Thondup, 2002, p. 123.

[81] Nyoshul Khenpo Jamyang Dorjé, 2005, pp. 319-320.

[82] Nyoshul Khenpo Jamyang Dorjé, 2005, pp. 320-322.

[83] *Terma* (Tib.; Wyl. *gter ma)* means treasure. *Terma* teachings are treasure teachings. A detailed explanation is given in Chapter 4.

[84] Nyoshul Khenpo Jamyang Dorjé, 2005, p. 321.

[85] Longchen Rabjam, 2002, p. 133.

and the testaments about his master's incarnations and was asked to keep it secret until the right time; and, he achieved the highest level of awareness when the five-colored light from his master's heart merged into him.[86] Without any signs of illness, Jigmé Trinlé Özer passed away into the supreme peace amid many miraculous signs, and a mass of relics after holy cremation was placed in a gilded stupa for the ordinary beings to pray and accumulate merits.[87]

The second Dodrupchen, Jigmé Phuntsok Jungné (1824-1863), was recognized according to the prophetic statements by Great Do Khyentse Yeshey Dorje. Jigmé Phuntsok Jungné studied under highly realized masters as Do Khyentse Yeshey Dorje, Dzogchen Mingyur Namkhai Dorje, and Patrul Rinpoche and achieved the highest realization through the path of great perfection. At the age of thirty, when a devastating smallpox epidemic hit the local population, he took the illness upon himself and died.[88] His guru Do Khyentse Yeshey Dorje came and gave the final instruction and asked, "Phuntsok Jungné, are you dead?" and kicked his body three times.[89] Then Jigmé Phuntsok Jungné sat up suddenly in meditation posture and remained in that state for a week without moving.[90] Countless awe-inspiring signs gave rise to deep faith.

The third Dodrupchen, Jigmé Tenpai Nyima (1865-1926), was born at Chak-khung as prophesied by Mingyur Namkhai Dorje.[91] His father was Dudjom Lingpa (1835-1904),[92] and his mother was

---

[86] Longchen Rabjam, 2002, pp. 133-135.

[87] Nyoshul Khenpo Jamyang Dorjé, 2005, p. 322.

[88] Nyoshul Khenpo Jamyang Dorjé, 2005, p. 232.

[89] Nyoshul Khenpo Jamyang Dorjé, 2005, p. 232.

[90] Nyoshul Khenpo Jamyang Dorjé, 2005, p. 232.

[91] Nyoshul Khenpo Jamyang Dorjé, 2005, pp. 323-324.

[92] Dudjom Lingpa was one of the greatest *Tertön* who revealed many *termas* known as Dudjom Tersar.The later reincarnations were Dudjom Rinpoche, Jikdrel Yeshe Dorje, and Dudjom Rinpoche, Sangye Pema Shepa.

Sonam Tso. Born amid marvellous signs with raised patterns of conch shells on the soles of his feet.[93] Frustrated with his inability to understand the spiritual texts in his childhood, Do Khyentse Yeshey Dorje appeared in his vision and blessed him, and after that, he could understand all the teachings and retain all of his guru's instructions.[94]

When Patrul Rinpoche requested teaching, the eight-year-old Jigmé Tenpai Nyima taught *Engaging in the Conduct of Bodhisattva*. The teaching inspired all his students and bought tears in their eyes that Dza Patrul Rinpoche was delighted and praised him, "Such teaching is not ordinary, but spiritual and given through the blessings of one's meditation deities. The fact that Dodrupchen, a child of eight, is capable of turning the wheel of the Dharma like this means that the period during which the teachings will endure is not yet over."[95]

Jigmé Tenpai Nyima studied with many great masters from the different Tibetan Buddhism schools without prejudice to be considered a great scholar. He received prophecies from his meditation deities in many visions, and three protective deities—Ekajati, Rahula, and Vajrasadhu—offered help and protection.[96] He was humble and shunned political power and personal fame, instead focused solely on the study, practice, and meditation throughout his life. He wrote dozens of valuable treaties that included prayers, advice, teachings, and pith instructions on *Dzogpa Chenpo*. At sixty-two, Jigmé Tenpai Nyima passed away without showing any sign of illness.

The fourth Dodrupchen, Jigmé Tubten Trinlé Palbar (b. 1927),

---

[93] Nyoshul Khenpo Jamyang Dorjé, 2005, p. 234. The sign of conch shells on soles is considered virtuous and auspicious.

[94] Nyoshul Khenpo Jamyang Dorjé, 2005, p. 324.

[95] Nyoshul Khenpo Jamyang Dorjé, 2005, p. 324.

[96] Nyoshul Khenpo Jamyang Dorjé, 2005, p. 325.

was prophesized and later recognized by the Great Fifth Dzogchen Rinpoche, Tubten Chökyi Dorje of Dzogchen Monastery, to be born to parents with the name Ka and Da.[97] As prophesized, his mother and father were Kali Kyi of the Kazhi clan and Drala of the Jekar clan respectively.

Figure 13. Kyabjé Dodrupchen Rinpoche.

Dodrupchen Rinpoche was born in 1927 in the Golok province of Dokham in eastern Tibet. There were many miraculous signs associated with his birth. Radiant light filled the entire house as Dodrupchen Rinpoche emerged from the womb; during the year he was conceived, a vague serpent-shape light would often enter the house and move along the walls; people saw the protective deity Rahula on the roof; a bird Raven Yalo with a broken beak and sacred

[97] Nyoshul Khenpo Jamyang Dorjé, 2005, p. 327.

to Dodrupchen Monastery flew over his house from time to time; and, flowers grew on the roof.[98]

At the age of four, Dodrupchen Rinpoche spoke spontaneously that he came from Zangdok Palri[99] and that Guru Padmasambhava lives there.[100] At fourteen, he fell seriously ill and went to see the guru Apang *Tertön*[101] for blessings and was in a retreat for one month to remove obstacles. He was reluctant to drink beer when Apang *Tertön* asked his attendant to serve but later thought: "Have I possibly interfered with the circumstances under which the guru might have ensured my spiritual attainment?"[102] After drinking without further hesitation, he experienced an indescribable, inconceivable, and ineffable state of realization of awareness that he could not communicate with the guru.[103] Apang *Tertön* told Dodrupchen Rinpoche to rely on Great Yukhok Jadralwa, an emanation of Omniscient Vimalamitra, as his teacher and to receive teachings from him.

At twenty-four during winter, Dodrupchen Rinpoche sat the feet of Yukhok Jadralwa to receive and practice the maturing empowerments, liberating instructions, and advice of the entire

---

[98] Nyoshul Khenpo Jamyang Dorjé, 2005, pp. 327-328.

[99] Zangdrok Palri is the holy residence of Guru Padmasambhava. Not accessible to ordinary human beings, only to highly realized practitioners of Guru Rinpoche. Many great *Dzogpa Chenpo* masters have vivid visions of visiting this place and receiving blessings directly from Guru Rinpoche.

[100] Nyoshul Khenpo Jamyang Dorjé, 2005, p. 329.

[101] *Tertöns* (Tib.; Wyl. *gter ston*; treasure revealers) were the designated accomplished masters with the responsibility of discovering the *terma* teachings hidden by Guru Rinpoche and Yeshé Tsogyal. The concise biographies of main *tertöns* are described in *The Nyingma School of Tibetan Buddhism: Its Fundamentals and History* by Dudjom Rinpoche, Jikdrel Yeshe Dorje (1991, pp. 743-869).

[102] Nyoshul Khenpo Jamyang Dorjé, 2005, p.330.

[103] Nyoshul Khenpo Jamyang Dorjé, 2005, p.330.

Dzogpa Chenpo approach of utter lucidity.[104] Motivated by personal experiences and guru's prophecies, at twenty-five, he set out to Derge to visit many monasteries and retreat centers and received many maturing empowerments and liberating instructions from many great masters.[105] His principal gurus were Yukhok Jadralwa, Jamyang Khyentse Chökyi Lodrö, and Khenpo Kunzang Palden.

In 1956, at age twenty-nine, Dodrupchen Rinpoche started receiving several prophecies from Guru Rinpoche about the attacks from the Chinese armies and to escape to the southern reaches of Bhutan.[106] On Saturday, October 12, 1957, he safely arrived in Gangtok, Sikkim in India, and since then made this seat his permanent residence. Under the request from the King of Sikkim Tashi Namgyal, Dodrupchen Rinpoche's accepted to conduct research work at the Namgyal Institute of Tibetology. His enlightened activities included the establishment of Chorten Monastery in Gangtok, where he instructs and guides hundreds of students and practitioners in the teachings of the Buddha. He continuously guides thousands around the world in the path of *Dzogpa Chenpo.* Being the principal lineage holder of Longchen Nyingtik teachings that his existence in this world is in itself a big blessing to all the sentient beings, particularly to followers of Nyingtik practice.

Shift to Taking a Refuge

In 2012, Khenpo Sonam, Mindroling Monastery in India, and I was fortunate to receive blessings from Kyabjé Dodrupchen Rinpoche in Chorten Monastery in Gangtok. As a personal assistant to Dodrupchen Rinpoche, Kunchog Yonten Lama accumulates enormous merits by

---

[104] Nyoshul Khenpo Jamyang Dorjé, 2005, p. 333.

[105] Nyoshul Khenpo Jamyang Dorjé, 2005, pp. 333-334.

[106] Nyoshul Khenpo Jamyang Dorjé, 2005, p. 335,

selflessly serving our guru—I offer my deepest gratitude to him. I would also like to thank him for providing guidance and assistance in receiving blessings from the guru.

Great Dodrupchen Rinpoche is the principal holder of Longchen Nyingtik teachings of the Great Perfection.[107] He is the Guru Rinpoche in the flesh. The blessings from Dodrupchen Rinpoche were another turning point in my life, my first significant step towards embarking on the Buddhist path. The boundless and compassionate blessings of an accomplished master are real and exist today.

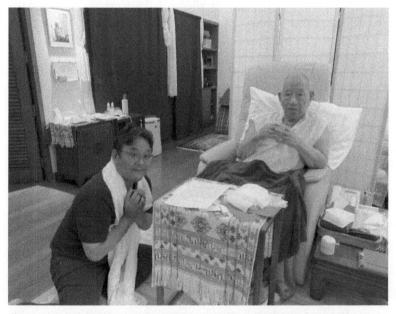

Figure 14. Receiving blessings from the Great Dodrupchen Rinpoche in 2019.

Slowly the shift turned from a momentary uneasiness to continuous edginess to put some extra effort into my practice. My limited

---

[107] Longchen Nyingtik is the heart-essence teachings of the Great Perfection. It was revealed by Great Rigdzin Jigmé Lingpa as mind treasure teaching.

Tibetan language added difficulty. Unable to read Tibetan *pecha* (Buddhist scripture), I relied on English translations.

I would like to thank all the translators for making valuable teachings of the Buddha available in English. Now English speakers can have free access to and free download of ancient Buddhist texts from 84000 website (http://84000.co/). The 84000 Project is translating the Words of the Buddha into English. It is a fantastic project initiated and led by Dzongsar Jamyang Khyentse Rinpoche, supported and managed by a professional team and experienced translators. It has touched and changed the lives of many people around the globe.

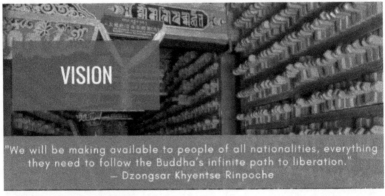

Figure 15. The vision of 84000 Project.

I attribute my more decisive shift for path-seeking to the blessings of Kyabjé Dodrupchen Rinpoche. Every opportunity to be in his presence is an excellent teaching in itself. His lucid expressions, serene composure, and compassionate gaze have the magnifying effect of sustaining my faith and devotion over the years.

Aspiring to follow in the footsteps of my master generates the motivation and discipline to start Buddhist practice seriously. His blessings also help to sustain my training. I received boundless compassion in his presence, although a few words were exchanged. It is self-evident that blessings are not transferred through words. His presence helped generate boundless faith and devotion, and I was fortunate to receive them on many occasions from 2012.

Lord Buddha best describes the speechless forms of blessings and realization. After achieving enlightenment, the Buddha's first words were: I found a truth that is profound, extremeless, luminous, uncompounded, but nobody is going to hear this. Therefore, I am going to remain in the forest without speaking. Dzongsar Jamyang Khyentse Rinpoche often explains that these words were the first profound teachings of Lord Buddha.

I was fortunate to receive the *lung*[108] of the Seven-Line Prayer from Kyabjé Dodrupchen Rinpoche in 2013 at Chorten Monastery. Receiving it from the living Guru Rinpoche was the ultimate blessings for the Seven-Line Prayer practice. With the blessings of the master, I have been following this practice diligently. When I told my parents, they were so contented. My father said, "Son, now I can die peacefully."

Path of the Seven-Line Prayer

The "Seven-Line Prayer (Wyl. *tshig bdun gsol debs*)" is one of the most powerful invocation prayers to Guru Rinpoche:

> "Hung
> In Orgyen's land, upon its northwest rim,
> On lotus, pistil-cup, and stem,

---

[108] Lung (Tib; Wyl. *lung*; oral transmission) is the oral transmission from a teacher to create an auspicious connection with the lineage of a particular text or practice. Then the student receives the blessings of the entire lineage which will help to understand the depth of the meanings.

Wondrous, supreme mastery you found
And as the Lotus-Born you are renowned.
A ring of many dākinīs encircles you,
And in your footsteps practicing we follow you.
To grant your blessings, come, we pray.
Guru Padma Siddhi Hung." [109]

I would recommend two books in English to understand the meanings of the Seven-Line Prayer. First, *The White Lotus*[110] by Great Jamgön Mipham Rinpoche.[111] Second, *The Sole Panacea*, a commentary based on *The White Lotus* by Kyabjé Thinley Norbu Rinpoche. These are useful reference books for the practitioners of this prayer.

The historical account of the origin of the great blessings of the Seven-Line Prayer:

"It is known as the prayer of wisdom Dākinīs inviting Padmasambhava for ganacakra offerings.[112] In the past, when Buddhism was flourishing in India, five hundred heretical teachers learned in grammar and logic came to debate with Buddhist scholars at Nālandā Temple to suppress the teachings of Buddhism. At that time, the Buddhist scholars could not compete with them. ... Dākinī[113] Mahāśāntidevī prophesied, "How can you defeat these heretics? My brother

---

[109] Padmakara Translation Group, 2016, p. 29.

[110] Tib.*tshig bdun gsol 'debs kyi rnam bshad Padma dkar po.*

[111] Great Jamgön Mipham Rinpoche is considered to be Mañjuśrī in human form.

[112] In Tantrayāna Buddhism, Ganacakra (Tib. *tshogs kyi 'khor lo*) is tantric assemblies or feasts accompanied by chanting matras, making offerings, and other tantric rituals.

[113] Dākinī (Tib. *Khandro* or *Khandroma*, Wyl. mkha' 'gro ma) literally means "female sky-goers". The title is used for sacred female deity in Vajrayāna Buddhism, and for female practitioners with high level of spiritual realization. It is explained in Chapter 4.

who is called Dorje Thötreng Tsal[114] is now staying in the charnel ground called Munpachen. If he is not invited to the debate, Buddhism will be destroyed." ... She thus taught the *Seven-Line Prayer*. As she had said, when they invoked him with the *Seven-Line Prayer*, Guru Rinpoche suddenly came from the sky. ... he defeated the five hundred heretics with logic and quotations. ... The heretics with evil intentions were destroyed by lightning and the rest were brought to Buddhism, and through Guru Rinpoche, Buddhism spread and flourished." [115]

In the 8th century, Guru Rinpoche bestowed this prayer to the King of Tibet and his subjects and later concealed the prayer as a profound treasure for the benefit of future beings of degenerate time.[116]

One can understand the prayer on outer, inner, and secret levels. The literal sense is explained in the outer level, the hidden meaning of the vajra words is unraveled in the inner level, and an explanation of how this prayer is implemented on the path in the secret level.[117]

Thinley Norbu Rinpoche explained the outer level of how to pray to Guru Padmasambhava:[118]

- Hung: The wisdom heart syllable of all Buddhas.
- Orgyen's land, upon its northwest rim: There is the country of Dākinīs known as Oddiyāna. On the northwest border of that place is a lake with water having great eight qualities. The lake is the manifestation of the wisdom Dākinī Mamaki appearing in the form of Dhanakosa Lake.

---

[114] Guru Rinpoche.
[115] Thinley Norbu, 2004, pp. 99-100. See Padmakara Translation Group, 2016, p. 25.
[116] Thinley Norbu, 2004, p. 100.
[117] Padmakar Translation Group, 2016, p. 26.
[118] Thinley Norbu, 2004, pp. 103-114.

- On lotus, pistil-cup, and stem: In the lake's center is a lotus flower rich with pollen. From the stem of this red lotus of the padma family in the center grow other lotuses with white, yellow, green, and deep blue colors—symbolizing the five wisdoms.

- Wondrous, supreme mastery you found And as the Lotus-Born you are renowned: When the time was right to subdue sentient beings, filled with the endless wisdom mind of Buddha Amitābha, Guru Padmasambhava—attained marvellous and supreme accomplishment—was instantly born from the heart of the red lotus like a sudden manifestation of awareness. Then one prays to Guru Padmasambhava with complete devotion.

- A ring of many Dākinīs encircles you: Many inconceivable Dākinīs surrounded Guru Padmasambhava.

- And in your footsteps practicing we follow you: I am following you with clear faith, enthusiastic faith, and confident faith from the bottom of my heart. I pray to you and practice to be like you.

- To grant your blessings, come, we pray: One should develop confidence in the teachings of Mahāsandhi and the view of all phenomena of samsāra and nirvana as just magical manifestations. Else one should believe with certainty that everything arises from interdependent cause and effect; that all beings are pervaded by Dharmakāya emptiness; that the minds of ordinary beings and Buddhas are the same. I pray to Mahaguru who is the refuge and protector of degenerate times from my heart that may my body immediately manifest as the empty bliss of Nirmānakāya[119] wisdom body

---

[119] Nirmānakāya is the body of manifestation aspect of Buddhahood.

and pureland; that may my speech immediately manifest as the empty clarity of Sambhogakāya[120] wisdom body and pureland; that may my mind immediately manifest as the empty awareness of Dharmakāya [121]wisdom body and pureland. I beseech you to immediately come to bless me.

- Guru Padma Siddhi Hung: The embodiment of the three kayas, Mahaguru, like a blossoming lotus flower that grows from the mud yet is unstained by it, your stainless wisdom mind never wavers from Dharmakāya wisdom, and you benefit beings through your beautiful splendourous arrays of wisdom bodies until samsāra is emptied. I pray to you to swiftly attain siddhis. The syllable Hung is the mantra that collects attainments, and all blessings are completely gathered.

Mipham Rinpoche explained the next level of inner meanings of the Seven-Line Prayers:[122]

- Hung: The see-syllable of the enlightened mind of the self-arisen primordial wisdom.
- Orgyen's land: This is the source of the Secret Mantra teachings, which is no other than the nature of our mind.
- Northwest: The west signifies samsāra, and the north refers to the pure state of nirvāṇa.
- Rim: This is the ultimate primordial ground (nature of mind) unaffected by either samsāra or nirvāṇa.

---

[120] Sambhogakāya is the luminous aspect of Buddhahood.
[121] Dharmakāya is the emptiness aspect of Buddhahood.
[122] Padmakara Translation Group, 2016, pp. 46-58.

- Lotus: It is emptiness, the ultimate expanse of primordial purity. Lotus or Buddha is the self-arisen wisdom, free from all attachments.
- Pistil-cup: It is naturally awareness wisdom, radiant, and in full flower.
- Stem: It holds both the lotus and the pistil-cup: the union of primordial wisdom and emptiness.
- And in your footsteps practicing we follow you: This means realizing with irreversible certainty about the ultimate reality, the primordial wisdom of the inseparable union of appearance and emptiness. By means of view, we become convinced of this ultimate reality; by means of meditation, we come to realize it; by means of natural manifestation of the naturally luminous primordial wisdom, all impure, ordinary perceptions will be transmuted into pure wisdom and will be blessed.
- To grant your blessings, come, we pray: We pray to express our aspiration for our mindstream to be blessed and the ultimate realisation of the ultimate reality may come to us.
- Guru Padma Siddhi Hung: The Guru is the empty nature of this primordial wisdom; the Padma is the expression of luminosity which is unstained by conventional attributes; the Siddhi is the indivisibility of these two is all-pervading compassion; and, the Hung is the seed-syllable of the enlightened mind and symbolizes the self-arisen primordial wisdom.

Mipham Rinpoche further expounded the final level of secret meanings of the Seven-Line Prayers:[123]

---

[123] Padmakara Translation Group, 2016, pp. 74-86.

- Hung: The supreme primordial wisdom.
- Orgyen: The land in which the Secret Mantra first arose. The Tibetan word for Oddiyāna (to fly and to progress). Fly away from the mire of samsāra with its dualistic appearances and make progress on the path.
- Northwest: The north represents the mind is freed or cleansed from the habitual patterns of samsāra, and the west, the mind is sunk in the mire of samsāra.
- Lotus, pistil-cup, and stem: The Lotus represents the enlightened speech where all sounds are purified; the pistil-cup, the enlightened mind where all the thoughts are perfected; and, the stem, enlightened body where all forms are impeccable. Receiving teachings on the enlightened speech, becoming convinced of the truth through reflections, absorbing them through meditation, and gaining the fruits of accomplishment: the four stages alluded by "lotus," pistil-cup," "stem," and "wondrous."
- Lotus-Born and renowned: The ultimate and spontaneously wisdom of Dharmakāya (pure, primordial nature of Buddhahood mind) arisen Lotus-Born and is renowned in limitless buddhafields in all directions.
- Many many dākinīs encircles you: All these appearances are the spontaneous display and projections of the ultimate nature of the mind.
- Footsteps and follow: With the view of the ultimate nature in mind, we practice in your footsteps and follow you.
- Grant your blessings: Pray to primordial wisdom to grant us blessings so that we might actualise this ultimate view.
- Guru Padma Siddhi Hung: The Guru is the essence of this path and highest of all wisdom; the Padma, the stainless primordial wisdom free from all attachment; the Siddhi,

actualisation of the final accomplishment; and, the Hung, the realisation of the inseparability of the ground and fruit indicated by the see-syllable of the mind of all the Buddhas.

The Seven-Line Prayer is a profound prayer that offers a complete Buddhist path. Even Mipham Rinpoche had expounded a Guru Yoga practice based solely on this prayer.[124] Despite all these wonderful insights, I still had to overcome the powerful and habitual adversary—laziness.

Laziness as an Obstacle

After receiving the oral transmission of the Seven-Line Prayer from Kyabjé Dodrupchen Rinpoche and under his continuous blessings, I started accumulating merits through the mantra recitation.

In this practice, a person counts the number of times a mantra has been recited. I could accomplish a limited number for 2013. It was not a diligent effort because I spent half-an-hour per day.

I had a pathetically slow start out of laziness and a casual attitude. It is not easy to become a diligent practitioner—not at all—my strong desire not to practice kept me away, that I used laziness as my excuse. After putting in considerable effort to overcome laziness, ultimately, I managed to become consistently diligent in my daily practice.

I decided to dedicate more time to my practice and to accumulate higher numbers. But that was not easy. I was in the middle of completing my Doctorate Thesis and had to attend to a full-time job. I was frequently on long-distance intercontinental business trips to Asia from Switzerland; implemented detailed planning of exhibitions, seminars, workshops, and training with Asian customers; involved in

124 Padmakara Translation Group, 2016, pp. 93-96. More on Guru Yoga practice in Chapter 5.

68

complicated and strategic decisions in fast-changing circumstances, requiring complex market analysis and communications with the different internal and external stakeholders. In this time-constrained situation, I had to develop an efficient time management system to handle all my responsibilities.

I was completely busy with my job for the whole day. After work, I spent a few hours on my thesis and dedicated the remaining hours until late at night for mantra recitation. On weekends, I spent more time on my thesis and sacrificed many outings and picnics with my family and friends. But I did attend some social activities because it is vital for physical and mental wellbeing. Such relaxing moments breathe fresh motivation and diligence.

Through this system, I was able to accumulate a lot more mantras in 2014. Whenever Kyabjé Dodrupchen Rinpoche blessed my mantra recitation, I was happy and satisfied, rekindling renewed enthusiasm and diligence in my practice—worthwhile efforts. Since then, I have been keeping good annual scores. Achieving it year in, year out requires immense dedication and diligence. I always pray to my Guru and Guru Rinpoche for their blessings to guide me to achieve my target every year until my death.

May I become a diligent practitioner and accumulate sufficient merits to realize this life as a dream—if not, at least be able to remember my master and Guru Rinpoche at the time of my death. Frankly, reaching such a level is made more challenging by the ubiquitous digital world with mobile apps and digital money.

Illusions of Mobile Apps and Digital Money

Nowadays, there are now many new methods of keeping you busy and occupied. The virtual world has so many interesting apps to keep you glued to your screens of smartphones, pads, laptops, TVs. Welcome to the world of illusions in the samsāra of apps.

Distractions and practice are competing for our time. More innovations in digital technology mean more hours of distractions— lesser time for prayers. The two examples of Hay Day and Bitcoin will show how we build illusory worlds.

The successful apps industry has witnessed tremendous growth and still growing. The app world is founded on the virtual wireless computing world, turning a virtual into a real-world. Its ludicrously powerful progress marked by acceptance of virtual-world-reality for almost all of us. We never question this phenomenon—instead accept it with great enthusiasm and confidence.

A person can spend hours, days, months, or even years glued to virtual apps. In some countries, like South Korea, playing virtual video games has become an addiction, even a disease.

In the Hay Day app, a person starts with a barren plot of land. First, planting wheat and corn in the fields; then produces flour from grain; later bakes bread from the flour and sells in the market. Buys some hens from the market. The hens have eggs. Sells them in the market and makes more money. With the additional income, buys some pigs to produce ham later.

In this cyclic phenomenon, the barren virtual farm turned into an elaborate imaginary world of reality, exquisite and attractive. The illusory farm does not exist—like a dream in cyberspace.

It is predicted in the future that we will live in this virtual world as one of the protagonists. It will not be far-fetched to imagine a person going on an Alaska winter sojourn physically in a virtual sense. The experience will be so close to reality that it will provide the same level of natural emotion. Despite the unreal virtual world, accepting the world as a dream is still a significant challenge for most of us.

Another latest phenomenon that caught my attention was the invention of a virtual currency called bitcoin. It's a virtual currency in the digital economy.

Figure 16. A farm in Hay Day (Left) and Bitcoin logo (Right).

In 2009, Santoshi Nakamoto released a white paper about the structure and working of an electronic cash system and launched the bitcoin network.[125] Bitcoin is an electronic payment system based on cryptographic proof allowing any two willing parties to transact directly with each other without the need for intermediary banks.[126] It is a cryptocurrency existing only in digital form. A person owns a personalized digital Bitcoin Wallet which stores all the bitcoins

The economic and financial experts predict that our future will be a digital economy using digital currencies similar to bitcoins. We can readily accept digital money but find it challenging to realize the illusory nature of life. I think that bitcoin is an excellent example to showcase the concept of the illusory nature of existence. Something that does not exist physically but exists virtually, a perfect union of existence and nonexistence simultaneously.

In summary, our habits are accumulated from numerous

---

[125] Nobody knows the real inventor of bitcoin. Whether it is Santoshi Nakamoto from Japan or a group of people?
[126] Nakamoto, 2009, p. 1.

eon—therefore, difficult to change. The distracting habits keep us away from Buddhist paths until a shift occurs. Then we take refuge in the Buddha Dharma. In Vajrayāna, we take refuge in a guru and follow the instructions diligently. During the process of practice, we might face the challenge of laziness. And the digital world of mobile apps and digital money helps keep us busy and occupied for hours. It makes me wonder if the digitzens will ever contemplate their real deaths—not a virtual death in the digital world!

Chapter 4

Death

Recognize everything in Bardo[127] as a projection of your mind:
Remember to pray to The Three Jewels when
living, dying, and after death.

Starting from China, the Coronavirus (COVID-19) pandemic spread across continents and has brought deaths of over a million and suffering to many millions more, affecting us like never before. This virus arrived suddenly without warnings leading to the closing and confinement of cities, schools, transportations, employment, and our daily lives.

The virus has shown that death can come to anybody, anytime and anywhere. This fact has been with us since our birth: universal fairness in our world. It does not differentiate between rich or poor, young or old, European or Asian. A moment of birth is the beginning of a dying process in Buddhism. Living is like dying slowly every day. Death is a big subject in Buddhism.

---

[127] Bardo is the intermediary state between death and rebirth. More detail and depth is given in the section "The Tibetan Book of the Dead" in this chapter. In Tibetan, the book is called *Bardo Thödol* (Wyl. *bar do thos grol*). This quote is the essence of the book and of Vajrayāna Buddhism.

Before discussing the details in *Bardo Thödol*, we need some fundamental understanding of the treasure teachings in Vajrayāna. Because it's a treasure teaching revealed by Great Karma Lingpa in the 14th century, learning about the *terma* tradition in Tibet and some of the great female revealers will provide a glimpse of the vibrant tradition that goes beyond gender and continues to survive and thrive.

Terma (Treasure) Teachings

One of the unique qualities of Vajrayāna is the existence of treasure teachings, more prevalent in the oldest Nyingma tradition of Tibetan Buddhism.

There are many *terma* mentioned in different Buddhist sūtras.[128] Many of them are still very actively taught and practiced amongst the practitioners.

Dudjom Rinpoche (1991) explained:

"During this defiled age their transmitted empowerments and instructions have become adulterated like milk in the market-place. Because [their lineages] have been interrupted by many lineage-holders, the fresh descents of their blessing have been weakened by many violations of the commitments, as well as by pollution [of the teachings] due to interpolations. But, regarding the contents of the treasures: The discoverers of treasure were emanations who had been drawn to following the great Padmasambhava of Oddiyāna himself, and had thus obtained complete transmission of

---

[128] Dudjom Rinpoche, Jikdrel Yeshe Dorje, 1991, pp. 743-745. The Buddhist sūtras about treasure teachings are Nāgarājapariprcchāsūtra, Āryasarvapunyasamuccayasamādhisūtra, and others.

the empowerments and instructions, which bring about maturation and liberation. By bringing forth in this way profound doctrines which embody the unfading, moist breath of the Dākinīs, they form close lineages, unequaled in the splendour of their blessings."[129]

In the 8th century, the lineages of *terma* were devised by Guru Rinpoche out of compassion for the future decadent times for *tertöns* to reveal them and propagate the Buddha Dharma.[130]

Guru Rinpoche and his close disciple Yeshé Tsogyal concealed an inconceivable number of treasure troves in upper, middle, and lower Tibet.[131] The responsibility of discovering these *terma* teachings was given to a few selected realized *tertöns*. These teachings were too early for transmission; therefore, they were concealed for future revelation at the appropriate time. Only the selected ones can decipher these *terma* teachings to maintain authenticity and create the basis for faith and devotion.

The *terma* tradition has two aspects: first, accomplished *tertöns* discover the teachings from the sky, mountains, lakes, trees; second, the gods, nāgas, and other powerful beings are the protectors of the teachings to be handed over to the right person at the proper time.[132] There are Earth, Mind, and Pure Vision *Terma*.[133] In the Earth category, *tertöns* can extract statues of Guru Rinpoche or relics from mountains, lakes, rocks, space. A *tertön* can transcribe volumes

[129] Dudjom Rinpoche, Jikdrel Yeshe Dorje, 1991, p. 745.

[130] Dudjom Rinpoche, 2003, pp. 34-35.

[131] Dudjom Rinpoche, Jikdrel Yeshe Dorje, 1991, p. 747. The many treasure troves were hidden in the western Tibet in Ngari and Tö, the central Tibet of Ü and Tsang, and the eastern Tibet of Kham and Amdo.

[132] Tulku Thondup Rinpoche, 1997, p. 57.

[133] For more detailed explanation of the types of *terma*, refer to Tulku Thondup Rinpoche's book, *Hidden Teachings of Tibet*.

of commentary, prayers, and practices out of their minds effortlessly like water flowing in a river. More than a dream, realized masters and practitioners have visions. From a vision, a *tertön* can transcribe all the instructions, teachings, and empowerments. They can also reveal relevant advice, prophecies, predictions for crucial times. The primary purpose is for the benefit of sentient beings.

Only the authentic *tertöns* are capable of revealing hidden treasure teachings. In the Nyingma Tradition, these *tertöns* are incarnations of realized disciples of Guru Rinpoche in their past lives. Except for a few *tertöns* who were celibate monks, most of them live in households with consorts (wives), children, and possessions. This non-celibate lifestyle is a practice to transform every source of experience in life to realization, not for sensory enjoyment.[134] A consort is a crucial means to realization and to discover the *Termas* by serving two purposes. Firstly, it helps to produce and maintain the wisdom of the union of great bliss and emptiness in tantric practice, and secondly, its mighty aspirations to help male *Tertöns* to discover profound esoteric teachings.[135]

The Dudjom *terma* lineage is one example of an unbroken line of highly accomplished masters: Dudjom Lingpa revealed it in the 19th century, Dudjom Rinpoche, Jikdrel Yeshe Dorje completed it in the 20th century, and Dudjom Yangsi Rinpoche, Sangye Pema Shepa helped to spread across the globe in the 21st century.

The Dudjom Yangsi Rinpoche explained in the *"A Brief History of the Troma Nagmo practice from the Dudjom Lineage"* article, "Contained within them are dozens of yidam[136] teachings, key instrument practices, and sādhanās.[137] Among these, the most

---

[134] Tulku Thondup Rinpoche, 1997, p. 82.

[135] Tulku Thondup Rinpoche, 1997, p. 82.

[136] In Vajrayāna, a yidam is a type of fully enlightened deity.

[137] Sādhanā (Skt.) generally means a spiritual practice.

effective and vastly beneficial practice for enabling practitioners to realize the attainment of a rainbow body is the teaching of Troma, the Black Wrathful Mother."[138]

The Troma Nagmo[139] esoteric teachings are a widespread practice in the Himalayan Bhutan and Nepal, also, by many practitioners in other countries. Dudjom Yangsi Rinpoche explained that "There were thirteen people who attained rainbow body along with Tragtung Dudjom Lingpa himself at Larung in Sertar (Larung Ngarik Nangten Lopling now)[140]. There were also many disciples in the lineage who attained rainbow body when Dudjom Lingpa was still alive ... The treasure also predicts that hundreds of thousands of practitioners will achieve the level of awareness holders by practicing this teaching in the future."[141]

Guru Rinpoche transmitted the *Terma* teachings for the benefit of future sentient beings.[142] His omniscience was that future generations would need potent instructions for our day and age: Troma Nagmo is one example. The power of the secret mantra will blaze like fire to counter the blazing fire of bad times, as prophesied by Guru Rinpoche.[143]

In the 8th century, the Great Tibetan female master Dākinī Yeshé Tsogyal helped Guru Rinpoche to conceal many *terma* teachings for future generations. It was through her blessings that we have a vibrant *terma* tradition alive. The instructions are like hidden medicines for future illnesses spiritually.

---

[138] Dudjom Rinpoche, Sangye Pema Shepa, 2019.

[139] Another name for Troma.

[140] It is located in Tibet.

[141] Dudjom Rinpoche, Sangye Pema Shepa, 2019.

[142] Tulku Thondup Rinpoche, 1997, p. 63.

[143] Dudjom Rinpoche, Jikdrel Yeshe Dorje, 1991, p. 935.

Ḍākinī (*Khandro*)

Current discussion about equal opportunities and pay for women in the 21ˢᵗ century cover so many aspects, including pay. A similar debate about gender equality took place in a remote north Indian city of Vaiśālī about 2,500 years ago recorded in The Vimalakīrti Sūtra at the time of Buddha Śākyamuni.[144]

Surprisingly, Tibet produced some of the prolific realized female Buddhist masters and practitioners in the form of *Khandro,* such as Khandro Yeshé Tsogyal (8ᵗʰ century), Sera Khandro (20ᵗʰ century), and Khandro Tāre Lhamo (21ˢᵗ century).

I decided to include this section under the subject of death with three main considerations. First, Khandro Yeshé Tsogyal was compassionate and instrumental in the concealment of invaluable *terma* in Tibet. Next, many *Khandromas*[145] played crucial roles in the restoration of Buddhism in Tibet after its destruction during the Cultural Revolution. Finally, to pay my homage, reverence, and gratification to all the past, present, and future *Khandromas.*

Being non-gender-specific, Ḍākinī means an individual who freely moves in the pure unlimited space of the panoramic wakefulness.[146] Ḍākinīs are the owners and protectors of Tantrayāna. They have been acting as the security locker in a private bank. Only the rightful holders have access keys to receive the precious tantric teachings from them.

The female has a significant role in Great Perfection. In the refuge practice, a female has a role equal to that of a male counterpart.

---

[144] 84000: Translating the Words of the Buddha, 2017, p. 70.
[145] Khandroma also means Khandro.
[146] Yeshé Tsogyal, 2017, p. 27.

Figure 17. The *kupar* of refuge tree in Longchen Nyingtik.

Based on primal wisdom, the essential nature of wisdom is emptiness, its natural expression is clarity, and its compassion is all-pervasive.[147] Guru Rinpoche with his consort Khandro Yeshé Tsogyal, both in white, sit at the center of the refuge tree. It's called Guru *Yab-Yum*.[148] In literal terms, *yab* means "father" and *yum*, "mother." The *yab-yum* means the tantric couple representing the union of "method and wisdom."[149] The *yum* represents the emptiness, and *yab*, the methods. Neither can exist without the other.

There is a tendency to leave out the contributions of women practitioners to the propagation of Tibetan Buddhism. However, in the Nyingma tradition, women have been active and vibrant as the consorts of prominent lamas and teachers.[150] In many cases, the female consorts are as respected as their male counterparts, exemplified by three extraordinary Tibetan female masters from the 8th to 21st century.

Khandro Yeshé Tsogyal (8th century)

Khandro Yeshé Tsogyal is Guru Rinpoche's voice; in fact, she is Guru Rinpoche in the feminine form: if Guru Rinpoche is the sun, she is the sun's rays.[151]

---

[147] Padmakara Translation Group, 1998, p. 177.

[148] Guru *yab-yum* (Tib.) is one such aspect of Vajrayāna that is grossly misinterpreted. The depth of its wisdom can only be appreciated after studying and understanding its true meanings.

[149] The yab-yum also means the union of form and emptiness as mentioned in the Prajna Paramita Sūtra. Method is *thabs* (Wyl.) and wisdom is *shes rab* (Wyl.) in Tibetan.

[150] Gayley, 2017, p. 7.

[151] Chönyi Drolma (2017, Trans.). Foreword. In *The Life and Visions of Yeshé Tsogyal: The Autobiography of the Great Wisdom Queen* (p. vii). Boulder: Snow Lion.

Figure 18. Mural of Yeshé Tsogyal in Samyé Monastery in Tibet from Jnanasukha Foundation, 2010.

Guru Rinpoche and Khandro Yeshé Tsogyal are the founding masters of the Nyingmapa and *Dzogpa Chenpo* lineage in Tibet. Yeshé Tsogyal is an embodiment of a pure and true tantrika who showed a path of devotion to guru in order to achieve enlightenment.

Widely depicted as the Tibetan consort of Guru Rinpoche,

Khandro Yeshé Tsogyal opened an indelible space for Tibetan women and raised their positions as accomplished masters in Vajrayāna Buddhism. She was Vajravārāhī[152] in human form and an emanation of Tārā.[153] There were many of her emanations in Tibet, including female tantrika such as Sera Khandro, Tāre Lhamo.

Tertön Drimé Kunga revealed the secret biography of Khandro Yeshé Tsogyal from an "earth treasure"[154] to benefit the future sentient beings by sharing her enlightened life as a source of inspiration and devotion.[155]

In this autobiography, Khandro Yeshé Tsogyal demonstrated how to be an excellent disciple who attained enlightenment in one lifetime.[156] You can also read about the life history of Yeshé Tsogyal in the *terma* discovered by Tertön Taksham Samten Lingpa that was later translated into English by the Padmakara Translation Group under the title *"Lady of the Lotus-Born, The Life and Enlightenment of Yeshe Tsogyal."*[157]

During her lifetime, Khandro Yeshé Tsogyal received, practiced, and concealed every teaching and empowerment into *termas* for future generations. She knew that future practitioners would need new teachings to keep them excited and motivated to pursue the Buddhist path. Yeshé Tsogyal's complete, unquestionable devotion

---

[152] Vajravārāhī (Skt; Tib. Dorje Pakmo; Wly. *Rdo rje phag mo*) is a wisdom dākinī who is the root of all emanations of Dākinī and depicted in red color.

[153] Tārā (Skt.; Tib. Drolma; Wyl. *sgrol ma*) is a popular female deity in Vajrayāna associated with compassion and enlightened activity.

[154] Earth *Terma.*

[155] Chönyi Drolma, 2017, Trans, p. 12.

[156] Chönyi Drolma (2017, Trans.). Translator's Introduction. In *The Life and Visions of Yeshé Tsogyal: The Autobiography of the Great Wisdom Queen* (p. 60). Boulder: Snow Lion.

[157] Padmakara Translation Group, 2012, Trans.

to Guru Rinpoche is the epitome of the Guru Yoga practice.[158] She is the perfect role model of this path to enlightenment, having achieved rainbow body at Zabbulung cave.[159]

Sera Khandro (1892-1940)

As an emanation of Khandro Yeshé Tsogyal, Sera Khandro Küsang Dekyong Chönyi Wangmo (popularly known as Sera Khandro, also as Dewé Dorjé) manifested not only as a Dākinī but also as a female *Tertön* during 1892 to 1940 in the barbaric[160] region of Golok. She came from a wealthy, politically powerful family in Lhasa.[161] Sera Khandro's father was Lhase Jampa Gonpo from Mongolian royalty, and her mother was Tsering Chodzom from the powerful Tibetan Nub clan.

Like Yeshé Tsogyal, Sera Khandro had an unswerving conviction and devotion to pursue a spiritual path from an early age. At seven in 1899, Sera Khandro revealed her first *terma*.[162] At eleven in 1903, she had a dream vision of Dākinī Vajrayoginī,[163] who gave her empowerments and profound teachings on channel and wind (Tib. *rtsa rlung*) meditation.[164]

When twelve in 1904, Dākinī Vajravarāhī appeared in her vision

---

[158] In simple terms, Guru Yoga means a practice of complete faith and devotion to a guru. The deeper meaning means uniting with guru's mind.

[159] Chönyi Drolma (2017, Trans.). Translator's Introduction. In *The Life and Visions of Yeshé Tsogyal: The Autobiography of the Great Wisdom Queen* (p. 51). Boulder: Snow Lion.

[160] Barbaric means a region that is like the Wild West.

[161] The capital city of Tibet.

[162] Jacoby, 2016, p. 34.

[163] Vajrayoginī (Skt.; Tib. dorje naljorma, Wyl. *rdo rje rnal 'byor ma*) is a wisdom dākinī depicted as red in color with a wrathful expression.

[164] Jacoby, 2016, p. 38.

and gave empowerments in the two cycles of *terma* teachings.[165] Sera Khandro was another perfect example of the Guru Yoga practice. When she saw her future guru Drimé Özer, son of Dudjom Lingpa, at the age of fourteen in Lhasa, tears welled up in her eyes, the hair on her body stood on end, and she prayed for compassion on her and never to separate from the guru for all the lifetimes.[166]

To pursue a spiritual path, Sera Khandro left the pleasure of her luxury life in Lhasa and escaped to follow Drimé Özer. She took the perilous journey to the wild and volatile land of Golok, which was known for banditry and marauding.

Only speaking Lhasa dialect[167] and without Golok's strong nomadic dialect, she found herself to be in an extremely precarious situation. Without food, shelter, and family protection, Sera Khandro had to work as a maid in a nomadic family to sustain herself in Golok. Many major obstacles came on her way to pursue the teachings from Drimé Özer. The consort Akyongza from a powerful family in Akyong Bum was a major obstacle and ensured Sera Khandro could never come close to Drimé Özer.[168]

During these turbulent times in Golok, Sera Khandro had a daughter and son from a rough marriage, and sadly the son died after birth. During these years, she continued to have visions of deities and revealed new treasure teachings. When Sera Khandro was twenty-three in 1915, Gotrül Rinpoche recognized her as a *Khandroma* and a *Tertön*.[169]

---

[165] Jacoby, 2016, p. 38.

[166] Jacoby, 2016, p. 39.

[167] Tibet has three major regions of U-Tsang, Kham, and Amdo. The Lhasa dialect is spoken in Lhasa in U-Tsang, and nomadic dialect of Golok is spoken in Kham.

[168] Jacoby, 2016, pp. 47-48.

[169] Jacoby, 2016, p. 58.

Figure 19. Sera Khandro painting in a nomad tent in Golok from Jnanasukha Foundation.

At twenty-nine in the fall of 1921 at Nyimalung, Drimé Özer performed a healing ritual for her failing health, and her condition gradually improved. She attained spiritual liberation and awakening through the union with her guru as male and female partners (*yab yum*) practice.[170] Together they revealed many treasure teachings, and their entourage of disciples expanded rapidly.

But crisis struck again in the form of plague in the Dartsang area in 1924. In the same year, at the age of thirty-two, Sera Khandro lost her five-year-old son and, three days later, lost her beloved guru Drimé Özer at the age of forty-three.[171] Even before the funeral proceedings had finished, Akyongza and her group expelled Sera Khandro and her daughter from the household.[172]

From the support of some of Drimé Özer's close disciples, Sera Khandro and her retinue found her new home in Sera Monastery in 1924. Her nickname "Sera Khandro," "the Dākinī of Sera," came from this place.[173] From here until her death, Sera Khandro turned into a prolific teacher giving empowerments and teachings to *tulkus*,[174] monks, nuns, kings, and laypersons. She repeatedly gave instructions of *terma* of Dudjom Lingpa, Drimé Özer, and her own.[175] Later, she became the lineage holder of these three lineages.

Sera Khandro completed compiling, copying, and editing the Treasures volumes of Dudjom Lingpa, Drimé Özer, and herself in 1933 and finished writing her long autobiography in 1934.[176] Finally, at forty-eight in June of 1940 at Riwoché, Sera Khandro passed into parinirvāna (Skt.):[177] As her disciple, Chatral Rinpoche described

[170] Jacoby, 2016, p. 63.
[171] Jacoby, 2016, p. 66.
[172] Jacoby, 2016, 66.
[173] Jacoby, 2016, p. 67.
[174] A *tulku* is the Tibetan word for a reincarnated Buddhist master.
[175] Jacoby, 2016, p. 68.
[176] Jacoby, 2016, p. 70.
[177] In Buddhism, parinirvāna refers to nirvāna-after-death. This term is used for only highly accomplished masters.

that the body of Sera Khandro had dissolved into light and shrunk to the size of a seven-year-old child.[178]

The hagiography of Sera Khandro is motivating and encouraging to path dwellers when facing perils or obstacles. Living in a family and diligently practicing Dharma is also touching. The complete faith and devotion to her guru show how to put Guru Yoga into practice, and her whole life is a profound teaching.

Khandro Tāre Lhamo (1938-2002)

Khandro Tāre Lhamo, a daughter of *Tertön* Apang Terchen Orgyan Trinle Lingpa (1895-1945), helped to revive the Nyingma Tradition of Tibetan Buddhism in Golok Kham, despite having suffered decades of manual labor under the Communist Chinese regime during Mao's Cultural Revolution, and despite the loss of her first husband Tulku Milo, the great-grandson of Dudjom Lingpa, her three brothers in prison, and her only son.[179]

On a pilgrimage to Lhasa when Khandro Tāre Lhamo was still an infant, Kyabjé Dudjom Rinpoche recognized her as an emanation of Yeshé Tsogyal and Sera Khandro.[180] Unlike Sera Khandro, Tāre Lhamo was born in a renowned Buddhist family of Apang *Tertön*. Therefore, she did not face the challenges of life as Sera Khandro did in the male-dominated religious milieu of Golok. But she witnessed the unimaginable destruction of Buddhism during the Cultural Revolution.

---

[178] Jacoby 2016, p. 74. This is another form of rainbow body. Therefore, Sera Khandro had achieved rainbow body after her death. To understand the entire autobiography of Sera Khandro, I would recommend you to read the book *"Love and Liberation"* by Sarah H. Jacoby.

[179] Gayley, 2017, p. 3.

[180] Gayley, 2017, p. 33.

Tāre Lhamo received ritual initiations from her father of the *Nyingtik Yabshi[181]* cycle and transmission of his entire treasure corpus.[182] Also, she received the oral instructions for the *Nyingtik Yabshi* from Rigdzin Jalu Dorje and Thubten Trinle Palzangpo.[183] During her lifetime, she had many visions. In one instant in early 1989, during a feast offering to the dākinī, she toured multiple dākinī lands and met the female deity Vajravārāhī[184] in person and realized the nondual bliss and emptiness.[185]

Tāre Lhamo was the Dākinī-in-action, performed miraculous feats on behalf of her local community, and revived Buddhism.[186] During the 1960s of the Great Leap Forward, she sojourned at night to celestial realms to bring back sacred substances to distribute and nourish those around her during the widespread famine.[187] Late at night, people came to Tāre Lhamo's tent on many occasions for *mo* [188] or *phowa*[189] for a deceased person.[190] She appeared in visions to male lamas in prison to console them and to predict their release.[191]

---

[181] One of the esoteric secret teachings of Dzogchen.

[182] Gayley, 2017, pp. 68-69.

[183] Gayley, 2017, p. 71.

[184] In Tibetan Buddhism, Vajravārāhī (Skt.; Tib. Dorje Phagmo, Wyl. rdo rje phag mo) is a wrathful form of Vajrayoginī. *Dorje* means that which is incapable of destruction, and *Phagmo* means the defilement of ignorance. Therefore, *Dorje Phagmo* means the transformation of ignorance into indestructible wisdom.

[185] Gayley, 2017, p. 72.

[186] Galey, 2017.

[187] Galey, 2017, p. 42.

[188] Divination.

[189] *Phowa* (Tib.; Wyl. *'pho ba*; Skt. utkrānti) is a ritual—and a practice—conducted by a Buddhist master directing the transference of consciousness at the time of death or for a dead person.

[190] Galey, 2017, p. 43.

[191] Gayley, 2017, pp. 73-74.

Figure 20. Tāre Lhamo with Namtrul Rinpoche. Original photo unknown.

In her second marriage to Namtrul Rinpoche, recognized as the fourth Namkhai Nyingpo emanation of Zhuchen Monastery in Sertar County, they contributed to the revitalization of Buddhism in Golok. They rebuild monasteries, donating funds, establishing ritual programs, and sponsored the construction of stupas, temples, and images.[192] They built a temple of Gesar[193] at the base of Amnye Machen outside of Tawu, the capital of Golok, and re-established the regional lore of King Gesar of Ling.[194]

As in the way Dudjom Rinpoche had recognized her as the reincarnation of Sera Khandro in Lhasa, Khandro Tāre Lhamo

---

[192] Galey, 2017, p. 44.

[193] The King Gesar of Ling (Ling Gesar) is a folk hero in the Eastern Tibet. In many parts of Kham and Amdo, the lore of the Epic of King Gesar is sung with deep faith and respect. My parents used to listen to it with great enthusiasm. They asked a good lore singer in Tibet to record the epic and send to them to Nepal. Ling Gesar is an emanation of Guru Rinpoche manifested in the form of a protective deity.

[194] Galey, 2017, p. 45.

in 1993 received the prophecy of the reincarnation of Dudjom Rinpoche in poems of dākinī scripts, translated them into Tibetan, and recognized Dudjom Yangsi Rinpoche, Sangye Pema Shepa as the reincarnated *Tulku*.[195]

Later, Dudjom Yangsi Rinpoche was recognized by Khenchen Jigme Phuntsok Rinpoche,[196] Dzongsar Jamyang Khyentse Rinpoche, Chatral Rinpoche, Thinley Norbu Rinpoche, Minling Trichen Rinpoche, Drubwang Penor Rinpoche, and many other renowned Tibetan Buddhist masters. In 1994, Chatral Rinpoche presided over the enthronement ceremony of Dudjom Yangsi Rinpoche in Godavari, Nepal, in the presence of twelve thousand people.[197]

It is so touching to witness how great masters like Chatral Rinpoche flawlessly and diligently preserved the *Dzogpa Chenpo* lineages and pass them completely to Dudjom Yangsi Rinpoche after fully training and making him ready to benefit sentient beings.[198] Now Dudjom Yangsi Rinpoche is extensively propagating the Buddha Dharma, particularly Dudjom Tersar, across the world.

---

[195] Rigpa Shedra, 2018.

[196] Kyabjé Khenchen Jigme Phuntsok Rinpoche (1933-2004) was one of the most renowned Buddhist masters of Nyingma Tradition of Tibetan Buddhism. He was the reincarnation of *Tertön* Sogyal Lerab Lingpa and an emanation of Miphan Rinpoche. During his life time, he revealed many *termas* in Tibet, Bhutan, China, Nepal, and India. After the Cultural Revolution, Khenchen Jigme Phuntsok Rinpoche played an extraordinary, extremely important role in the revival of Buddhism in Tibet. To sustain the future growth of Buddhism in Tibet and China, in 1980, he established one of the non-sectarian, largest, and famous Buddhist institutes locally known as Larung Gar in Sertar in Eastern Tibet.

[197] Chatral Rinpoche, 2007, p. 77.

[198] Chatral Rinpoche, 2007, p. 72.

Figure 21. Tāre Lhamo and Namtrul Rinpoche with Dudjom Yangsi. Original photo unknown.

On March 26, 2002, Khandro Tāre Lhamo passed into parinirvāna in a hospital in Chengdu, the capital of Sichuan Province: "... in her final hour, Tāre Lhamo lay down in a resting posture. Many lamas, including Khenpo Jigme Phuntsok and Dodrupchen Rinpoche, called to recite prayers for her over the phone. Before she passed away, as recounted, she smiled and looked vibrant as if she were twenty years old. ... inside the building, there was a perfume scent, and rainbow clouds of various colors also appeared all around, inside and outside. ... When it was cremated, her last testament reports that rainbow light filled the sky and pieces of vulture feather fell to earth."[199]

A fascinating continuity of her lineage, Khandro Tāre Lhamo has taken birth in the family of her father's reincarnation His Holiness the

---

[199] Gayley (2017).Epilogue. In *Love Letters from Golok: A Tantric Couple in Modern Tibet* (p. 262). New York: Columbia University Press.

forty-first The Sakya Trichen, Kyabgon Gongma Trichen Rinpoche, the head of the Sakya tradition of Tibetan Buddhism from 1951 to 2017. She has reincarnated in female form as Jetsun Kunga Trinley Palter, a granddaughter of Sakya Trichen, on January 2, 2007 in India.[200] Indeed, her lineage and treasure teachings will continue to thrive in the 21st century.[201] Also, I hope to have more female Buddhist teachers in the future who will enjoy the same religious and social status as their male counterparts in our societies. In this, Khandro Tāre Lhamo has given us a good start!

From Dākinī Tāre Lhamo to my chance meeting with David Gration, it was a pleasant experience to my book-writing journey for many good reasons.

Chance Meeting with David Gration

In life, some events happen by fate. My meeting with David Gration was one of them.

On the evening of July 13, 2019, I was tour guiding my Taiwanese friend Professor Dr. Rusty Hsieh in Zürich. After walking through the old town, we decided to take a short break for cold beer inside the Zürich Main Station and to witness the hustle and bustle of hundreds of crisscrossing local and international travelers.

Only a few days before, my wife Yangchen and I had discussed retired Professor Dr. David Gration, my Doctorate Thesis Adviser. I said "I was thinking of him to be the editor of my book, but having lost contact since 2014, the chances of this happening were remote."

---

[200] Gayley (2017).Epilogue. In *Love Letters from Golok: A Tantric Couple in Modern Tibet* (p. 277). New York: Columbia University Press.

[201] If you are excited and fascinated to read all about how Khandro Tāre Lhamo restored and revived Buddhism in Golok, I would recommend Holly Gayley's book *Love Letters from Golok: A Tantric Couple in Modern Tibet.*

Figure 22. Meeting with my mentor David Gration on July 13, 2019.

Suddenly, I saw David Gration in front of my eyes as he walked towards the TV Monitor to check his next train back to Geneva. He was with his granddaughter and family members of her fiancé. I walked briskly to greet him. With a surprised expression, David told me that he had mentioned me to the group an hour ago as they also strolled through the old town (as somebody who knows a lot about India). He was pleased to accept my offer for a glass of beer. Rusty, David, and I talked while sipping local beer.

We updated each other about many things that have happened in our lives since 2014. During our conversation, I briefly mentioned the book that I was writing in which death was one of the main themes. His eyes filled with curiosity, and I asked him if he would like to be the editor of my book. In his early eighties, David keenly accepted the proposal adding that he had close encounters with death. Chapter 4: Death would be the first section of the book I passed him to read.

David had some concerns, being an atheist and with limited knowledge about Vajrayāna Buddhism. On the contrary, I thought a dialogue between a Vajrayāna path-seeker and an atheist could be interesting. I was excited to explore what might come out of this interaction. With the promise to meet again soon, we said au revoir as David boarded the train to Geneva. Was it a chance meeting, coincidence, or fate? I think it was all three: happy outcome.

Next day, I sent a draft of the chapter on "Death" to David. Death was close to us for different reasons: David had near-death experiences, and I had recently lost both my parents.

Fourth Distraction: Death

Death is a Distraction in two aspects: its unpredictable nature and its unrealized occurrence.

How naïve to think that death cannot come tomorrow! Long-term planning for future careers, children's education, retirement, pension, wills, funeral, and so on. Unconsciously, we are aware of our slow dying process every millisecond. The painless subtle happening fails to create an alarming impact like a lethal car accident. Slowly but surely, we become more assured and accustomed to believing that death will not come tomorrow, particularly young people— rather than the old and terminally sick. The young and healthy prefer to think that they will not die soon. If that happens, the young are shocked and alarmed. Reluctantly, we acknowledge that death can come at any age and anytime.

During a month-long holiday in December in a cozy and luxurious five-star beach resort in Bali, Europeans have fun and excitement in the beginning. In the end, the same persons become conscious of returning to stressful, hectic lifestyles in cold weather to face the most dreadful boss for another long year. Only when the fun is over, do we realize the suffering of the lost holiday?

Likewise, we become conscious of death only when it shows its ghastly appearance in COVID-19 or cancer. Otherwise, we have become numb to the slow dying process. Willingly, we continue to remain distracted, assuming that it will not come in the next moment. Some Tibetan masters would empty their cups and leave them upside down when going to bed at night because they are never sure whether they would wake up the next morning to use them.[202]

Becoming consciously aware of the death process is a vast subject in Vajrayāna Buddhism. There are a complete path and practice in *The Tibetan Book of the Dead* for both living and dying.

The Tibetan Book of the Dead, living consciously, dying consciously

The *Bardo Thödol* is initially written in Tibetan and translated as *The Tibetan Book of the Dead* in English.[203] It was discovered as a *terma* teaching by a 14th-century *tertön* Karma Lingpa.[204] The first translation of the book into English was by Lāma Kazi Dawa-Samdup in 1927, edited by W.Y. Evans-Wentz. Since then, many translations and commentaries have become available.

I was fortunate with the opportunity to study the *Bardo Thödol*'s teachings with Khenpo Sonam from Mindroling Monastery, India, during his three-month-long stay in Switzerland. I will share my understanding of its vast teachings using specialized terms to

[202] Sogyal Rinpoche, 1994, p. 22.
[203] Dudjom Rinpoche (2003, pp. 61-75) has written an introduction to the Bardo in the *Counsels from My Heart.*
[204] Dudjom Rinpoche, Jikdrel Yeshe Dorje, 1991, pp. 800-801.

describe *Bardo*, and the non-Buddhists can comprehend this section as a dying process behind the jargon.

Bardo means the experience between death and birth. *"Bar"* represents in between, and *"do"* means island or landmarks between two things.[205] The period between confusion and the confusion that is just about to be transformed into wisdom.[206]

This typical teaching of living and dying consciously comes from the Nyingma lineage, where death has never been negative because one will never appreciate life without death.[207] The *bardo* teachings are not only for the dead but also more importantly, for the living.

There are six types of *bardo*:

    (1) *Bardo* of birth and life,[208]

    (2) *Bardo* of the dream,[209]

    (3) *Bardo* of meditation,[210]

    (4) *Bardo* of the moment of death,[211]

    (5) *Bardo* of the luminosity of the true nature,[212] and

    (6) *Bardo* of becoming.[213]

---

[205] Fremantle and Chögyam Trungpa, 1987, p. 10.

[206] Fremantle and Chögyam Trungpa, 1987, pp. 10-11.

[207] Dzongsar Jamyang Khyentse, 2011a.

[208] Tib. *Kyenay bardo*; Wyl. *skye gnas bar do*. This *bardo* is from conception to death.

[209] Tib. *Milam bardo*; Wyl. *rmi lam bar do*.

[210] Tib. *Samten bardo*; Wyl. *bsam gtan bar do*. This *bardo* is experienced by meditators.

[211] Tib. *Chikhai bardo*; Wyl. *chi khai bar do*. This *bardo* occurs when external and internal breaths are terminated.

[212] Tib. *Chonyi bardo*; Wyl. *chos nyid bar do*. This *bardo* starts when the peaceful and wrathful deities appear in the form of clear lights.

[213] Tib. *Sipa Le Kyi bardo*; Wyl. *srid pa las kyi bar do*. This *bardo* is determined by the karma for next birth.

The first three *bardos* are reasonably self-explanatory. Therefore, I will write something about the last three *Bardos*.

According to Buddhism, we are made up of five elements: wind, earth, water, fire, and space. When we die, these five elements dissolve into consciousness, consciousness into space, and space into luminosity.

In the fourth *Bardo* of the moment of death, the different stages a person goes through before reaching the final death are:[214]

Stages	Elements	Signs	Remarks
1	Dissolution of wind element.	Difficulty in digestion and a slow loss of body warmth from downwards, forgetting things quickly, difficulty controlling emotions, loss of appetite, and difficulty in using limbs.	The initial stage of death, and the end of the gross wind element.
2	The earth element dissolves into the water element.	The strength of the body degenerates, the skin becomes dry, and the teeth will have an abnormal stain. The mind becomes very obscure, forgets simple things, and depression will arise. The body becomes heavy and asks to lift the body. Start to see lots of mirages everywhere.	Visualise the guru inside your heart and pray.
3	The water element dissolves into the fire element.	The moisture of the body drys, nostrils become drown in, and the tongue gets twisted. The mind feels hazy, nervous, and irritated. Experience smoke-like mist.	Visualise the guru on the navel and pray.

---

[214] Dzongsar Jamyang Khyentse 2011b-2011m.

4	The fire element dissolves into the wind element.	Breathing becomes chilly, the warmth of the body fades, and steam rises from the head. The mind becomes very clear like a child and suddenly does not remember its name and experience millions of fireflies.	Visualise the guru on the forehead and pray.
5	The wind element dissolves into consciousness.	Choking starts, long in and out breaths, noisy breathing, and eyes turn upwards. Mind completely confused and see different visions. Experience a strong flaming torch.	Visualise the guru on top of the head and pray. This is the time when we call it death. In *Bardo* teachings, a person is still believed to be alive, and we are recommended not to touch the body.
6	The consciousness will dissolve into space.	Outer breath stops.	Clinically dead.
7	A white drop falls from the head.[215]	Thirty-three conceptions of anger stop.	Experience of a clear moon.
8	A red drop arises from the navel.[216]	Forty conceptions of attachment and desire stop.	Experience of a bright red.
9	Pervading luminosity between white and red drops.	Seven subtle conceptions of ignorance stop.	Experience of blackness.

Table 1. Described by Dzongsar Jamyang Khyentse Rinpoche.

---

[215] A white drop represent the male semen.
[216] A red drop represents the female egg.

DEATH

Unlike the Christian concept of a soul, Buddhists believe that all the effects of karma (causes, conditions, and results) are stored in the *'alaya'* and carried into the next life. The *alaya* continues but is always changing according to your actions.

In this lifetime, if you have a strong propensity for anger, particularly while you are dying, the impact of this negative emotion may well continue into your next life.[217] On the other hand, if you have trained your mind in mindfulness, love, compassion, or strong bodhichitta, the positive memory of this mind training will remain intact in your next life.[218]

After Stage 9, there arises a bright light that is the true nature of your mind. The accomplished masters or experienced meditators will recognize it and rest in *thuktam* as explained by Kyabjé Dudjom Rinpoche:

> "If a person has achieved stability in the recognition of luminosity during meditation, then as soon as the experience of untarnished space arises, there occurs the so-called meeting of the mother and child luminosities, space and awareness. This is liberation. At root, this is what lamas and meditators who practice refer to as "resting in *thuktam*," or meditation, at the time of death. *Thuktam* is nothing more than this."[219]

When a deceased person fails to recognize the bright light, the fifth *Bardo* of the luminosity arises. The peaceful and wrathful deities of the five Buddha families will manifest. Although there are no

---

[217] Dzongsar Jamyang Khyentse, 2018b, p. 93.

[218] Dzongsar Jamyang Khyentse, 2018b, p. 93.

[219] Dudjom Rinpoche, 2003, pp. 66-67.

99

sensory organs, the *bardo* being can have sharper sensations for being in a state of its innate mind.

The forty-two peaceful deities will appear for the next seven days starting from Buddha Vairocana, Buddha Aksobhya, Buddha Ratnasambhava, Buddha Amitābha, and Buddha Amoghasiddhi. At this stage, the *bardo* goes through a reverse of samsaric experience that is the perception of light and images that are in intangible states of quality instead of tangible form in the living world.[220]

The different colors represent different Buddha families and human emotions: white for Buddha Vairocana and ignorance, blue for Buddha Aksobhya and hatred, yellow for Buddha Ratnasambhava and pride, red for Buddha Amitābha and desire, and green for Buddha Amoghasiddhi and envy.

On the first day, the vision that appears is Buddha Vairocana in white holding a wheel symbolizing ignorance; on the second day, Buddha Aksobhya appears in blue holding a Vajra personifying hatred; on the third day, Buddha Ratnasambhava appears in yellow holding a gem representing pride; in the fourth day, Buddha Amitābha appears in red holding a lotus epitomizing desire; in the fifth day, Buddha Amoghasiddhi appears in green holding a crossed vajra symbolizing envy; in the sixth day, all the forty-two peaceful Buddhas will appear with the four guardians of the gates, the four goddesses, and the six realms of the world simultaneously; in the seventh day, the vidyadharas that are neither peaceful nor wrathful but intermediary, impressive, overpowering, and majestic appear, at the same time, a dim green light of the animal realm appears.[221] Don't go after the green light; else, you will be reborn in the animal realm.

---

[220] Fremantle and Chögyam Trungpa, 1987, p. 15.

[221] Fremantle and Chögyam Trungpa, 1987, pp. 15-24. Vidyadhara means holder of knowledge or insight. They represent the divine form of the tantric guru.

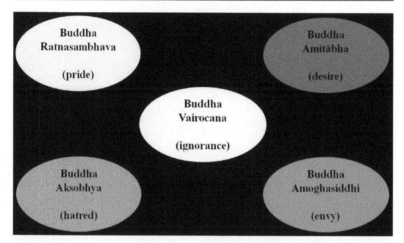

Figure 23. Relationship between the five Buddha families and different emotions.[222]

Guru Rinpoche advised a *Bardo* being to realize everything as the projection of one's mind, to develop faith, and prayer to all the Buddhas with complete faith and devotion.

From the eighth until twelfth day, the peaceful Buddhas are now transformed into wrathful Herukas[223] and their consorts in dramatic forms with three heads and six arms.[224] The five peaceful Buddha families become Buddha Heruka, Vajra Heruka, Ratna Heruka, Padma Heruka, and Karma Heruka with their respective consorts.[225] In essence, the peaceful and wrathful deities represent fear and hope: fear in the sense of irritation because the ego can't manipulate them in any way, and hope in a perpetual creative situation as primary neutral energy, neither good nor bad.[226] The end of the twelfth day marks the end of the *Bardo* of luminosity.

---

[222] Fremantle and Chögyam Trungpa, 1987, pp. xviii-xix.

[223] Heruka (Skt; Wyl. *he ru ka* Tib. *khrag 'thung*) is another name for enlightened deity in wrathful form.

[224] Fremantle and Chögyam Trungpa, p. 24.

[225] Fremantle and Chögyam Trungpa, pp. 25-26.

[226] Fremantle and Chögyam Trungpa, p. 26.

Figure 24. This *Zhitro Thangka*[227] was painted by Pema Namdol Thaye[228] using hand-ground earth pigments and semi-precious stones and 24k gold. It was completed in 2018 after more than twelve months of intense focus to encompass all one hundred peaceful and wrathful deities and Guru Padmasambhava and his two consorts along with the three Dharma protectors. The artist used his twenty-five years of studying, painting, and sculpting *Zhitro* deities according to the *Zhitro* text and the personal instructions given by his master Venerable Lama Gonpo Tenzing Rinpoche and Kyabjé Chatral Rinpoche.

The thirteenth day marks the beginning of the *Bardo* of becoming until forty-nine days. Out of the seven weeks, the first three weeks are crucial because the deceased has the same perceptions they had during life.[229]

Once again, Guru Rinpoche gave a lot of advice to a *Bardo* being. At all times, remember that everything is the projections of your mind. Call out and pray to the root guru or deity or Buddha or three jewels. Recollect good merits accumulated during your lifetime. Meditate upon your guru. Look into the nature of fear and recognize its empty nature. Try to remember the teachings of *Bardo Thödol*.

The ultimate goal is liberation. If that is not possible, a *Bardo* being should try not to be reborn in the three lower realms (animal, hell, and ghost realms) and hope to take rebirth in one of the three upper realms (heaven, asura, and human realms). In Buddhism, a human form is the most precious of the six realms because it provides the optimal causes and conditions to practice the Buddha Dharma.

---

[227] *Thangka* (Tib.; Wyl thang ka) is a hanging scroll depicting a Buddha or highly realized masters.

[228] Pema Namdol Thaye has won international acclaim as a master of traditional Tibetan arts. He is a painter, 3-D mandala specialist, traditional Tibetan architect, art educator, author, and the founder of Padma Studios®. Highly innovative, Pema's work has been exhibited in museums and galleries through the United States, Europe, and Asia, including the Victoria and Albert Museum (London), Rubin Museum (New York), and the Asian Art Museum (San Francisco). For more information, please visit www.PadmaStudios.com.

[229] Dudjom Rinpoche, 2003, p. 72.

The moment of death offers excellent potential for liberation. When the mind separates from the body, everyone experiences the nakedness of our Buddha nature, and liberation is achieved upon recognizing this nature.[230]

As death draws near, try to give up your worldly concerns: stop worrying about your family, stop making plans, stop thinking about what you haven't managed to accomplish, stop thinking about all the appointments in your diary.[231] Tantrikas should tell their guru and close spiritual friends who may offer spiritual help and support during the dying process and beyond.[232] Think and contemplate about bodhichitta frequently by generating the desire to make others happy.[233] Finally, you should follow the example of a wounded deer and retire to a solitary place to die.[234]

While living, a person should realize that life and death are the mind's projections like an illusory dream. This will help to make death seem like a nightmare. Another method is to convince yourself that you will die during the night and pray to be reborn in the Buddha Amitābha realm; in the next morning, remember to see all the phenomenal existence as temporary: a practice for Buddhists, agnostics, atheists, and those who care for the dying.[235]

Out of boundless compassion, Guru Rinpoche gave precious helpful advice to *Bardo* beings during the *Bardo* of the luminosity of the true nature and the *Bardo* of becoming:

- Realize all the different experiences from ignorance, hate, pride, desire, and jealousy are the projections of your mind;

---

[230] Dzongsar Jamyang Khyentse, 2018b, pp. 51-52.

[231] Dzongsar Jamyang Khyentse, 2018b, p. 54.

[232] Dzongsar Jamyang Khyentse, 2018b, p. 54.

[233] Dzongsar Jamyang Khyetntse, 2018b, pp. 55-56.

[234] Dzongsar Jamyang Khyentse, 2018b, p. 54.

[235] Dzongsar Jamyang Khyentse, 2018b, p. 58.

- Recall your root guru, Guru Rinpoche, Kandro Yeshé Tsogyal, Chenrezig, the three jewels, and any other deities you worshipped in your previous life;
- Offer all the beautiful places or flowers or mellows to the three jewels;
- Remember the empty nature of all things;
- Remember all the empowerments during your lifetime;
- See all beings in your *Bardo* as Buddhas;
- All colors of a rainbow as your guru;
- Remember the *Bardo Thödol* if you had read or received its empowerment;
- When witnessing sexual intercourse, see them as male and female deities in a *yab-yum* posture;[236]
- Whenever possible, meditate upon the nature of your mind as introduced by your guru. Dudjom Rinpoche mentioned that recalling your guru is more powerful and quicker than anything else because you have had met and built a relationship with your guru.

A word of caution here. If a *Bardo* being had not heard or contemplated or practiced the teachings of *Bardo Thödol*, the chances of exercising this advice will be difficult. The only way is to practice the Dharma in this life. The *Bardo* of birth and life is the most crucial because one can practice the Dharma in this life. This will help to recognize everything as the projection of our minds during the *Bardo* journey.[237]

To learn about the *bardo* teachings, read *The Bardo Thödol* by Karma Lingpa in Tibetan and its English translation, and

---

[236] In most of the Tibetan *Thangka*, many of the deities are painted in a *yab-yum* posture representing the union of emptiness (*yum*, female deity) and form (*yab*, male deity).
[237] Dudjom Rinpoche, 2003, p. 73.

commentaries by Chögyam Trungpa Rinpoche and Dzongsar Jamyang Khentse Rinpoche.[238]

Buddhist Rituals as a Boat

In Vajrayāna Buddhism, we have many religious pūjā.[239] Tibetans are quite fond of doing *shaptens* and *mo*, a form of divination. There are many divination forms: one is through consultation with a revered lama and another through consultation with a deity. It is recommended to do the divination through a master or deity to whom you have complete faith and devotion.

My parents always did annual *mo* for the whole family or specific problem through Kyabjé Chatral Rinpoche. Then Chatral Rinpoche advised us to conduct certain types of *shapten* to remove future obstacles.

On one occasion in 1995, Chatral Ripoche advised me not to go to any crowded places or big events for the whole year and advised many *shaptens*. I followed the instructions earnestly, also recommended by my parents. Consequently, I faced no significant obstacles throughout the year. As an offer of reverence to my parents, I continue to carry forward our family tradition of doing annual *shaptens* of *Dolma Doncho*,[240] *Boom*,[241] and *Zhitro*[242].

I have a positive karmic connection with *Zhitro*. During one of my visits to Nepal in the nineties, my father woke up early in the

---

[238] The details are given in the bibliography.

[239] Pūjā (Skt.; Tib. *shapten*) means reverence, honor, homage, adoration and worship. It is used mostly for worship rituals these days.

[240] *Dolma Doncho* is the pūjā to a female deity Tārā.

[241] *Boom* is pūjā that includes reading the words of the Buddha.

[242] *Zhitro* (Tib. shyitro; Wyl. zhi khro; Zhi means peaceful and tro, wrathful deities) pūjā is the recitation of the main text from the *Bardo Thödol* (The Tibetan Book of the Dead).

morning. He took a taxi from Boudhanath to *Yangleshö* to receive blessings from Chatral Rinpoche and an offering for *Zhitro* Pūjā. Chatral Rinpoche had told my father to bring me along the next early morning for *Zhitro Wang.*[243]

When my father asked to come along the next morning, I opted for longer sleep hours instead of Zhitro *Wang*. Later my father told me that Chatral Rinpoche did ask about me. Chatral Rinpoche and Dudjom Yangsi Rinpoches had prepared the empowerment for both of us. My father was lucky but I wasn't. Even today I have deep regret to have missed the marvelous opportunity. But the compassionate realised masters sowed the seeds of future karmic connection. Later, it was their blessings that created the causes and conditions to study and contemplate the teachings of *Bardo Thödol* and also received *Zhitro Wang.*

In 2017, my father was bedridden and paralyzed. When I was taking care of my father in Nepal, we heard the arrival of Dudjom Yangsi Rinpoche. The Rinpoche was very kind to give *Zhitro Wang* to my father. When nearing death, it is very beneficial to receive *Zhitro Wang* from a realized master to whom a person has unwavering faith and devotion. My father had both towards Dudjom Yangsi Rinpoche. I was fortunate to receive it along with other family members. This fulfilled the karmic link to the blessings of *Bardo Thödol*.

Death is a Great Teacher

Death feels real when you experience it. Unlike hearing from the radio or watching on TV. I experienced deep sorrow and pain at the deaths of my father and mother.

I could not attend the funeral after my father died on December

---

[243] *Zhitro Wang* means the empowerment of *Zhitro*.

3, 2016. My siblings, relatives, and friends in Nepal organized all the pūjās including cremation.

I regret not being with both my parents when they died, for practical reasons. But I feel less pain to know that both were terminally ill. The death of my father took a while to seep into my psyche. Whenever I thought about him, I realized the loss was forever. Not be able to share my thoughts with him anymore hurts me deeply.

The death of my mother on April 27, 2017, was more dramatic! Because I participated in the whole proceedings. Not as a distant bereavement.

I witnessed the traditional Tibetan way of venerating the dead. The first thing is to consult a Tibetan lama about the details of a funeral. Accordingly, we prepared the entire funeral and performed the rituals for forty-nine days to help my mother as she passed through different stages of *Bardo*.

The cremation date was a few days after her death. So we kept her body in our home. We wrapped it up in a white cloth and drew four rectangles on the area of the fabric covering her face. Two small rectangles on the first row, one rectangle on the second and third rows, the same length as the smaller two.

Figure 25. Butter lamps and pūjā for forty-nine days for my mother.

We put a portrait of her guru and lit the butter lamps on a table next to her head. Because of the lamps, we kept her door open all the time. When I opened the door of my room in the morning, I saw through the door opening a cold, lifeless, dead body of my mother lying in her room. I felt the impermanence of our existence. A few days ago, she was alive and talking, and now lying motionless and speechless. Consciousness never dies, a key reason why Tibetans handle the dead with respect. Because consciousness experiences all human emotions a thousand times amplified, our aim of pūjās is to provide some guidance and direction during the *Bardo* journey.

Unlike in the west, cremations in Nepal are carried out in the open, making them more visible and dramatic.

On May 1, 2017, I felt a series of intense, dramatic emotions when I laid my mother's dead body on the funeral pyres to lighting the fire.

I saw the fire burnt all the traces of her existence forever by turning them into ashes. The loss of her presence was real. I have never felt death so concrete, and the elimination of existential reality was tragic. Suddenly I realized the significance of sharing your thoughts and emotions with your parents when they are still alive. You can't share your opinions with them once they turned into ashes.

Unable to share when your parents are alive, you will live your remaining life with unspoken words and unshared emotions. This will torment you. Instead of regretting, I would recommend you to say aspiration prayers for departed souls. Buddhists can accumulate immense merit by praying that all the *Bardo* beings recognize experiences as projections of their minds.

Death helped to develop respect and admiration for this moment to live, and faith and determination to practice the Dharma. Death is a supreme teacher of impermanence.

Figure 26. Funeral of my mother on May 1, 2017, in Nepal.

The *Bardo* teachings helped me to face death with a positive attitude and handled the funeral proceedings with seriousness and veneration. We invited monks from monasteries, where our mother had closer associations. We lit butter lamps and recited *Zhitro* with love, conviction, and prayers for all living, dying, and dead.

Today, the deaths and sufferings caused by the COVID-19 pandemic have shown the impermanence of our existence and the inevitability of death. To Buddhist practitioners, it reminds them to practice the Dharma with greater urgency and diligence. It is a healing process for our sick minds to accept death, transform our attitude towards life, and realize the connection between life and death.[244]

Acknowledging that we are dying every day is a good start. But even more important is to remember the love, care, and compassion of our parents. When they are old and still alive, reciprocate them with more love and compassion. Visit your parents in nursing homes

---

[244] Sogyal Rinpoche, 1994, p. 31.

or old people's homes, and present them with flowers and chocolates, and have lunches or dinners with them. Spend time with them more frequently. Say to them how important they are in your lives and how much you appreciate and love them. Make them feel precious!

I feel deep sorrow when I hear sad episodes from many of my friends working in old people's homes in Switzerland about old fathers or mothers waiting for their children the whole day. I earnestly appreciate the gracious gestures of some of my friends who gave flowers to them on behalf of their children. At least, the disguised blessings produced an excellent sleep.

Despite all the adversaries and deaths, the incredible Tibetan *Khandromas* sought the blessings of their gurus with unwavering faith and devotion. When Guru Rinpoche was about to leave Tibet, Khandro Yeshé Tsogyal requested concise and easy-to-practice teaching at the time of death. The compassionate master said don't be fascinated, don't doubt, and don't be afraid of whatever fearful phenomena that will appear in the forms of sounds, colors, and lights because all of them are the manifestations of your mind.[245] These instructions show the importance of faith and devotion in a Buddhist path to achieve liberation from samsāra.

---

[245] Erik Pema Kunsang, 1999, pp. 153-157. Khandro Yeshé Tsogyal concealed this teaching as a *terma* teaching for the future generations.

Chapter 5

Devotion

Those with faith will go for refuge;
Those who have compassion will have bodhichitta;
Those with wisdom will gain realization;
Those who have devotion harvest blessings.[246]

Faith and devotion will give rise to wisdom, compassion, and blessings. As the devotion to Buddha is an actual practice, the unwavering faith and devotion to a guru will produce faster blessings because, unlike Buddha, in this lifetime, we have met the guru, with whom developed a personal connection, and from whom we have received teachings and empowerments. In Vajrayāna, a guru is the embodiment of all the Buddhas because we received all the instructions and blessings through the guru — a quintessential Guru Yoga practice.

Speed is the hallmark of our times, even when it is not necessary. We seek rapid results in politics, economy, education, innovation, and other aspects of our lives. Because time is limited and valuable, there is a tendency to go for speedy methods. There is nothing wrong with "speed." But more often than not, we focus on quantity rather

---

[246] Dudjom Rinpoche, 2003, p. 28.

than quality. In business, as in life, a healthy quantity-quality balance results in more sustainable outcomes. For example, as parents, we want our children to grow faster and more competitive—even more than they would like to be. We push our seventeen-year-old son Tsering to behave like an adult, forgetting he is still a teenager. Not reminding ourselves how we were at that age nor asking ourselves whether Tsering will be happy or not. An unhappy childhood will have a lasting negative impact more than rapid academic success and maturity.

To achieve speed and efficiency, people seek quick-fix solutions and faster return on investments: simply, more results in a shorter period. Efficiency is doing things well, while effectiveness is doing the right things well. It is better to be effective than efficient when quick-fix solutions lead to more re-fixing later. Ultimately, consuming more time rather than saving time. A modern age assumption that time is in scarcity often tempts people to opt for efficiency than effectiveness, perhaps achieving neither

Another example of effectiveness is how European countries and the USA, during the initial stages of the COVID-19 pandemic, chose business over safety. Many nations decided to keep the borders open for commercial activities when the virus was rapidly spreading, with unknown new variants emerging. It was an easy decision to keep the business afloat. In hindsight, this has proven fatally wrong. The right decision was to lock the borders down, equipping all the hospitals and healthcare workers for the future upsurge of patients, and educating the public to wear face cover and follow social distancing in public gatherings: saving tens of thousands of unnecessary deaths.

As an example of a scarcity of time, the modern electronic gadgets with 5G connection and social media keep us busy to stay in constant touch with the world. These innovative products make our world so comfortable that getting śūnyatā into minds is all the more difficult. All these leave people with limited time for practicing the Dharma. Shockingly, TV advertising sells fast cars shown blatantly breaking the speed limits and driven recklessly—luring all the speed lovers—although we have the choice to drive reasonably or take the safety and relaxation of the train.

It would be great if all Buddhists can follow the comprehensive Buddhist path of reading, hearing, contemplating, and meditating. In the presence of deep attachment to our families, this distraction is one of the most difficult challenges because of strong intimate emotions and social responsibilities.

Fifth Distraction: Family Attachment

Usually, after having achieved some professional success, people settle down to raise a family. The new family becomes one of the strongest attachments in our lives, taking center stage in our existence.

Husbands or wives become closer than parents, and children more valuable than siblings. Keeping happy with both your past and present family members becomes harder. We try to rebalance and to find an acceptable equilibrium of relationships. Not easy to achieve since we are now more emotionally attached to wives and children.

In this evolving relationship, the inclusion of Buddha Dharma adds another layer of complexity. Focusing on family relationships while also devoting time and energy to a Buddhist practice is not easy, especially with a young family. If not managed well, this could create destructive cracks in the family, even breakups, leading to more stress. Not a good option. But there are ways and means to combine family and practice.

A right approach would be to discuss this matter more openly and frequently with your family members to gain their understanding and cooperation. Having good support from your family is conducive to a healthy practice of Dharma. Forcefully choosing Dharma over the family would lead to painful separation and is not necessary. In case of a long retreat for a few months or years, it is important to openly discuss with your wife or partner and children about the appropriate timing. Choosing the time of least negative financial and emotional impact is an excellent consideration. Bringing all the family members on board to consensus will create not only harmony but also more generous support in the future. Your family will provide the necessary support for your practice.

In Buddha Dharma, the practice is more important than family to achieve the ultimate liberation. But most of us are not determined enough to abandon the family in pursuit of wisdom like the great masters of the past. We lack the grit to completely give up our families for seeking the truth—considered inhumane and socially unacceptable. So it is still much more comfortable and better to maintain an amicable family relationship and practice the Dharma simultaneously.

A person must become more creative in selecting the Dharma path that is feasible and suitable for individual and family needs. For me, faith and devotion to the gurus and aspirational prayers have worked well for many reasons.

Firstly, through the Seven-Line Prayers' blessings, I could develop faith and devotion to my master. The lack of Buddhist knowledge is not a handicap. I enjoy reciting aspirational prayers for their soothing poetry and am motivated to practice for their grand aspirations. I am merely reciting with diligence and consistency, two essential virtues for practice.

Secondly, due to my busy professional career, I cannot spend lots of time reading, hearing, and contemplating the words of the Buddha. A remedy is by being selective in what to read, hear, and contemplate.

The choice of your reading depends upon the path you are choosing. My readings are more in the areas of Mahayana, *Dzogpa Chenpo*, and Longchen Nyingtik. Fascinated by the teachings' depth, from the blessings of the translations, I can read many teachings in English.

Thirdly, I read many hagiographies such as Lord Buddha Śākyamuni, precious Guru Rinpoche, Khandro Yeshé Tsogyal, and other great masters. Their efforts, dedication, sacrifices, and aspirations provide the necessary fuel to my practice. They have proven that the ultimate liberation from samsāra is possible, even in one lifetime.

Finally, the transparent discussions with my wife and son and their understanding and support offered the space and time to dedicate adequate time to my practice. Some of our traditional pilgrimages to India and Nepal and receiving blessings from great masters strengthened our mutual respect and responsibilities to support each other in this spiritual journey.

We aim to have a healthy family bonding that provides suitable conditions for practicing the Dharma. Each family can practice as a husband, wife, father, mother, son, daughter, lawyer, business person, doctor, professor, billionaire. Or seek a renunciation path and become a monk or nun in a monastery or a practitioner in a hermitage. Non-practicing Buddhists need not worry because you will find a suitable path from 84,000 paths taught by the Lord Buddha.

Moreover, I sincerely pray that all the path-seekers can find an appropriate and sustainable balance between family and Dharma. May none of you have family breakups or financial problems. May all of your family members become genuine path-seekers and practitioners.

The Vimalakīrti Sūtra

There is a fascinating and relevant-to-modern-world Mahayana Vimalakīrti Nirdeśa[247] Sūtra, commonly known as The Vimalakīrti Sūtra.[248] The most captivating theme of this sūtra is about a layperson called Vimalakīrti falling sick.

Vimalakīrti, who belonged to the Licchavi clan in the current Bihar, an eastern state in India, was one of the most successful business tycoons and a famous citizen in his region at the time of Buddha Śākyamuni, and truly an accomplished master of profligate excess.[249] He perfectly personified a union of pride and generosity. His wisdom teachings are mind-boggling when meeting with some of the greatest saints of that time.

When discussing with Lord Buddha's closest disciple Śāriputra about meditation, Vimalakīrti said that true meditation is to mediate and not mediate simultaneously; to be mindful and active at the same time, and is not to stop doing things.[250]

In another instance with another Lord Buddha's closest disciple Maudgalyāna, Vimalakīrti mentioned that everything is an illusion, including the path that liberates us from delusion; the path is the teaching; therefore, teaching, hearing, understanding, and realizing are all illusions.[251]

On another occasion, Vimalakīrti expounded on compassion with Kāśyapa, one of Lord Buddha's greatest monk disciples whom Buddha himself has appointed to be his regent, Vimalakīrti said that

---

[247] Nirdeśa (Skt.) means "instructions, advice."

[248] I read the version translated by 84000: Translating the Words of the Buddha, 2017. You can download it for free at https://read.84000.co/translation/toh176.html.

[249] 8400: Translating the Words of the Buddha, 2017, p. 8.

[250] 84000: Translating the Words of the Buddha, 2017, p. 15.

[251] 84000: Translating the Words of the Buddha, 2017, p. 20.

everyone – the rich and the poor, the famous and the insignificant – should be equally objects of compassion.[252]

One day, Vimalakīrti told Rāhula, the only son of Lord Buddha, that a true renunciant must renounce not only all causes but also all results: renounce not only worldly life but also the benefits of becoming a monk or a nun.[253]

There are so many unimaginable events explained in The Vimalakīrti Sūtra that I could not list them all here. You should read the text to explore many more such episodes of immense learning. But let me conclude with the question from Lord Buddha to Vimalakīrti about how he viewed the Buddha.

On the absolute level, Vimalakīrti said that Buddha is beyond form, beyond feeling, beyond karmic formation, beyond symbol, beyond time; Buddha is not darkness, not the illumination, not a name, not a mark, not a reference, not powerful, not weak; Buddha has no form, no eyes, no ears, no gender, and so on.[254] The teaching is similar to the Prajna Paramita Sūtra about form and emptiness, samsāra and śūnyatā.

Accomplished Vimalakīrti is sharing the essence of Buddhism in this sūtra. In most cases, we will never experience such a realization in this lifetime but reading about it only fills us with great aspiration and encouragement that such realization is achievable at the end of a path.

Such a possibility is an immense motivation to a path-seeker like me. At a mundane level, it is fascinating to learn that a magnate — like Vimalakīrti — can be a great Buddhist practitioner and sets as a role model for laypeople to practice Dharma seriously.

It took some time for me to work out how to balance family life

---

[252] 84000: Translating the Words of the Buddha, 2017, p. 23.

[253] 84000: Translating the Words of the Buddha, 2017, p. 27.

[254] 84000: Translating the Words of the Buddha, 2017, p. 82.

and practice. I used to think that to practice Buddhism, one must leave the family and go to a mountain and meditate in isolation for years. After becoming a path-seeker, I learned that many paths allow people to live ordinary family lives in union with Dharma practice. The Vimalakīrti Sūtra confirms that such paths are feasible and will also lead to an ultimate realization of wisdom.

Speedy Methods

In this century, we are looking for speedy paths with quicker returns. For example, instant messaging apps demand instant communication and replies. Even emails have become too slow now—although emails allow us to read, think, react, and reply promptly. The problem lies more with human demands than technology. To further speed up communication, people created new jargon of acronyms such as lol (laugh out loud), brb (be right back), btw (by the way), lmk (let me know), g2g (got to go), ama (ask me anything), and many more. This trend, despised by many linguists, is irresistible to younger generations and will continue to grow in the future.

Similarly, in Buddhism, the faster methods are those that can bring more rapid results. All of us are different. None has the same spiritual aptitude and sharpness to grasp Buddha Dharma's wisdom. Master Patrul Rinpoche said that a genuine, realized master would provide a path according to mental capacity. All the 84,000 teachings of the Buddha are to tame the minds from getting distracted from endless thoughts. The Vimalakīrti Sūtra demonstrates that enlightenment is possible using any methods whatsoever.[255]

Not all skillful methods work for everyone. What works for one person might not work for another. With the right approach to the right person, under suitable conditions, the correct result is

---

[255] 84000: Translating the Words of the Buddha, 2017, p. 91.

achieved.[256] This is cause-condition-result in action. In Tantrayāna, there are plenty of skillful methods to help practitioners to realize the truth, at times, even using negative emotions as methods of practice.

My father described an interesting method used by Kyabjé Polu Khen Rinpoche to help his disciples become aware of their thoughts:

"Once Polu Khen Rinpoche and some of his disciples—including I—were roaming around in the holy pilgrimage site of Rajgir in Bihar, India.[257] They were on a pilgrimage and survived on alms and begging. During the daytime, Polu Khen Rinpoche asked all his disciples to roam in the jungle to collect beads from the Bodhi tree. They used beads to make Bodhi mālā[258] for reciting the mantra.[259] While searching and collecting the beads from the ground, the guru instructed them to speak aloud whatever thoughts came to their minds, everything and anything. The purpose of this practice was to make all of us realize what was going through our minds. Without paying any attention, many thoughts racing unknowingly, ceaselessly through our minds at all times. When speaking aloud, I realized this phenomenon and became more conscious of the constant waves of thoughts passing through my mind."

---

[256] 84000: Translating the Words of the Buddha, 2017, p. 92.

[257] Rajgir is considered to be a holy site for Buddhists. It is located in the state of Bihar in India. One of the most visited pilgrimage site is "The Vulture Peak." Here Buddha Śākyamuni preached the wisdom teachings of Prajnaparamita. I really don't remember the exact dates of this event, and can only surmise the period to be in ninety sixties.

[258] Mālā (Skt.) is also known as rosary.

[259] My parents mentioned to me that Bodhi Mālā is very good for reciting the Seven Line Prayer.

I found this episode quite exciting and funny. Interesting because we often avoid talking to ourselves and rarely aloud. Funny to imagine what Indian herders in the jungle thought about Tibetan people dressed in different attire and speaking a foreign, unrecognizable language, most likely took them as madpeople. In the end, my father found this to be an effective method to look into his thoughts.

The method that I find useful is taking notice of my emotions. Anger is one of the easiest to detect due to its imminent visibility. Its entrance is bold, loud, imposing, overpowering. Reminding myself, when I could, about the arrival of anger helps to weaken its reprisal. At the beginning of practice, the intensity of rage will not diminish at all but over the period, once getting more conscious of this negative emotion, its power will weaken.

Another example is in the moment of joy, looking at the autumn leaves. The mild cold of autumn has taken over the warm summer as reflected in the turning colors of beautiful trees. The leaves are so splendid that many Japanese will visit Kyoto to enjoy its autumn glory. While basking in the sight of these leaves, I try to remind myself about the bygone summer and the impermanence of time and life. Soon the autumn will also leave us giving way to cold, snowy winter. But let us not be overwhelmed by melancholy autumn days. Instead, enjoy its beauty with a pinch of impermanence: the union of beauty and unpredictability.

Now I believe that devotion to Dharma is an effective method to achieve faster results. In the treasure text of *The Wrathful Guru*[260] revealed by Great Terdag Lingpa, Guru Rinpoche said that if you wish for swift accomplishment and special blessings, make offerings and meditate on me the Lotus-Born.[261] Devotion does not cost money

---

[260] *The Wrathful Guru* (Tib. *bla ma drag po*).
[261] Padmakara Translation Group, 2007, p. 44.

and time but requires practice to develop this habit: build faith in the Buddha's teachings and develop devotion to your guru as the embodiment of all the qualities of a Buddha.

When we are lazy and suffering from limited time for practice, or surrounded by entertaining distractions, use methods that bear quick results. After becoming a devoted practitioner, these challenges are no more limiting excuses. The biggest challenge is how to get motivated to start a serious practice of faith and devotion and sustain it for the rest of our lives because our dualistic mind makes it harder to develop complete devotion to a guru.

Dualistic Mind

The path of faith and devotion is not without problems for modern people. Asking for 100% faith in a master raises eyebrows these days. Our "objective mind" will immediately give rise to many critical queries: Why should I trust this master? Is this a realized master? Can I achieve some realization following this master? How can he be like a Buddha?

The skepticism will continue to increase. Our smart, curious minds are capable of producing more questions than answers. These are valid questions to which there are no easy answers. Buddha said that the absolute truth (wisdom) is beyond speech and experienced only through practice.

Many great masters frequently teach us that after a certain period of analysis in path-seeking, one must stop any further investigation and engage in a path of faith and devotion. Otherwise, one will spend the entire life, most likely, in study and analysis rather than practice. In short, go beyond the dualistic analysis.

Taking the past as a reference, we should follow in the footsteps of great practitioners who achieved high realization in this path.

Patrul Rinpoche recorded many successful cases in *The Words of My Perfect Teacher* and some that I have witnessed in my limited lifespan. I have seen many highly realized Dzogchen masters who are solely concern about the liberation of all sentient beings and spent their entire lives, out of absolute compassion, sharing their acquired wisdom with others.

In this path, one must develop total confidence in the Dharma, seek a genuine master, and follow the guru diligently with complete faith and devotion. These are the prerequisites in the Guru Yoga practice; without it, there is no realization.

Guru Yoga: Devotion to Your Guru

In Vajrayāna, the practice of remembering the guru is of great significance—the essence of the Guru Yoga[262] practice. Guru Yoga is the practice of merging one's mind with the wisdom mind of the master.[263] The word "Yoga" is not limited to only physical exercise, a widespread misunderstanding. In the Guru Yoga context, it is purely a mind training to realize the ultimate wisdom. It is so vital that no one has achieved liberation from samsāra without relying on a guru.[264]

In this practice, a person follows a realized guru; develops pure perceptions of the guru as a living Buddha in human form; evokes a deep faith and devotion for the blessings; mixes one's mind with the mind of guru; and, finally realizes the absolute truth.[265]

The most profound practice is mixing your mind with your

---

[262] Guru Yoga (Skt. guruyoga; Tib lamé naljor; Wyl. bla ma'i rnal 'byor).

[263] Rigpa Shedra, 2014.

[264] Padmakara Translation Group, 1998, p. 312; Drubwang Penor Rinpoche, 2017, p. 97.

[265] Padmakara Translation Group, 1998, pp. 309-347; Dzongsar Jamyang Khyentse, 2012, pp. 177-190.

guru's with fervent devotion all the time until you attain perfect Buddhahood.[266] The essence of the "mixing" process includes our entire body, speech, and mind.[267] The word mixing could be misleading because it seems to imply that there are two different entities. But, the point is that the two minds have never been separated.

Developing pure perception is another pre-eminent practice in receiving the blessing from your guru. Thinking and remembering the guru frequently is like thinking of the Buddha, and bringing your guru to mind is the same as remembering the true nature of your mind.[268] The calling to the guru is the most effective mindfulness practice. Patrul Rinpoche reaffirms the unimaginable blessings to think about one's teacher for a single moment.[269]

There are many records of immediate realization through the practice of Guru Yoga. The Tilopa-Nāropa anecdotal case fascinates me. Great Nāropa (1016-1100) was a highly learned master and scholar of the famous Buddhist University of Vikramaśīla[270] in ancient India. On the other hand, Tilopa (988-1069) was a great wandering tantric and meditation master who made his living by grinding sesame seeds.

Following the advice from a wisdom dākinī, Nāropa went in search of his guru Tilopa and then started following all the instructions from his master. To realise the true nature of mind, Tilopa hit Nāropa on his head one day, and instantly Nāropa's wisdom became identical to his master.[271] In our skeptical world

[266] Drubwang Penor Rinpoche, 2017, p. 98.

[267] Dzongsar Jamyang Khyentse, 2012, p. 179.

[268] Dzongsar Jamyang Khyentse, 2012, p. 59.

[269] Padmakara Translation Group, 1998, p. 310.

[270] The three great monastic universities in the ancient India were Vikramaśīla, Nālandā, and Odantapurī.

[271] Padmakara Translation Group, 1998, p. 312.

today, our education system will accuse Great Tilopa of misusing his teacher's position and authority. Although outwardly crazy, it was the beginning of the highest realization in Mahāmudrā[272] and the start of the excellent meditation lineage in the Kagyü school of Tibetan Buddhism.

The Guru Yoga practice is not a one-way-street relationship from disciple to the guru; instead, it is a journey of the practitioner seeking refuge, blessings from the guru, and guru offering selfless guidance and effective methods to realize the ultimate wisdom. It is a complicated relationship based on total transparency, commitment, diligence, and honesty—a journey of togetherness.

There are many signs of maturity in a practitioner. A practitioner will develop purer perceptions of others than a beginner; become more humble; incite greater devotion to the guru; diminish pride and arrogance more quickly; and, the supreme sign is the loss of interest in material gain, fame, the respect of others, or being the center of attention.[273]

For a busy modern person, the Guru Yoga practice can be a reasonably handy and effective way to realize the truth. But our analytical habit becomes the biggest obstacle.

Even after taking refuge in a guru, we often continue with our analysis. For example, you will doubt your pure perceptions of your guru when the guru bursts out in anger. One will ask, "How can my guru become angry? And Why?" Instantly, the foundation of the pure perception of a guru falters, and the practice collapses. The antidote is to think that our dualistic mind is visualizing the guru in such a manner. One of the fundamental prerequisite mindsets in

---

[272] Mahāmudrā (Skt.; Tib. *Chakgya Chenpo*; Wyl. *phyag rgya chen po*; also called the Great Seal) is the meditation tradition of the Kagyü school of Tibetan Buddhism.
[273] Dzongsar Jamyang Khyentse, 2012, pp. 186-187.

the Guru Yoga practice is to stop any analysis of guru. If you have doubts about your guru, it will be difficult to receive the blessings.[274]

Reading, hearing, and contemplating the Buddha's words are significant building blocks for a strong devotional path. For the same reasons, why Ngöndro practice is so crucial for safer passage through. In *The Words of My Perfect Teacher*, during Ngöndro practice, a path-seeker learns about the impermanence of life, the sufferings of samsāra, the principle of cause and effect, the benefits of liberation, the taking of refuge, the arousing of bodhicitta, the cleansing of obscurations, the accumulation of merits, the Guru Yoga practice, and the instructions for the dying. Like applying manure and water to the soil for seeds to grow, the Ngöndro practices prepare students to become effective in the Guru Yoga path. In a nutshell, devotion is all about trusting in the phenomenon of cause-condition-result.

Omniscient Longchenpa said that it is essential to rely on a guru to direct your mind towards the spiritual practice of past masters and raise your level of experience and realization. Guru Yoga is one of the most potent methods to realise the true nature of the mind. Master Jamgön Mipham Rinpoche expounded a Guru Yoga practice based on the Seven-Line Prayer.[275] Many past practitioners have chanted this prayer with strong faith and devotion and realized the true nature of the mind.

Accumulating Merits

Our Buddha-nature is a wish-fulfilling gem like a blue sky showing itself once dark clouds have vanished. Our defilements are the clouds, and accumulating merits are methods to eliminate them. The Buddha-nature will manifest once our karmic obscurations are

[274] Drubwang Penor Rinpoche, 2017, p. 98.
[275] Padmakara Translation Group, 2016, pp. 93-96.

purified and sufficient merits accumulated.[276] It is crucial to start accumulating merits without procrastination.

There are many different ways to achieve merit—every ordinary event in our lives can be transformed into a source of merit. For example, when you see a beautiful flower at the market or in the hills, you can mentally offer them to the Three Jewels so that the experience becomes meaningful and thus accumulate merit.[277] Likewise, you can visualize offering your food to the hundred deities in your body mandala.[278]

Other examples, we can dedicate our compassion to distressed refugees by offering to all those similar fate to be able to find a safe place to live and raise their family in peace, love, and harmony. To dedicate the ordinary act of spending time with the old and sick can be transformed into earning merit by offering it to all the similar people in this world; may they find loving and compassionate caretakers throughout their remaining years. To dedicate at work, managers delegating fairly and appropriately to improve staff development and their career prospects to all the workers around the world; may people always find bosses who are fair, honest, caring, and compassionate.

Even adverse incidents as sickness or failure can provide opportunities for merit. Pray to the Three Jewels that such disease or loss may not occur to all the sentient beings—may there be good health and success. The significance of using daily activities is always to remind ourselves about the Dharma.[279] Being conscious and aware of the Dharma all the time is essential in Buddhist practice.

---

[276] Drubwang Penor Rinpoche, 2017, p. 87.

[277] Drubwang Penor Rinpoche, 2017, p. 88.

[278] Drubwang Penor Rinpoche, 2017, p. 88. According to *The Tibetan Book of the Dead*, our body is a mandala of hundred deities.

[279] Drubwang Penor Rinpoche, 2017, p. 89.

We should make offerings with pure motivation—not out of miserliness or self-pride—and conclude it by dedicating the merit to all the sentient beings. The offering of lamps helps to purify the obscurations of ignorance, and according to Dzogchen, it develops and increases inner wisdom.[280]

One of the immense merits is making offerings to one's guru. With complete faith and devotion, offering a bouquet can accumulate merits greater than providing food to a thousand Buddhas because your guru introduced you to your Buddha-nature. Therefore, a practitioner should use every opportunity to make offerings to the master.

On an auspicious Dākinī Day of July 27, 2019, in Bangkok, I was fortunate to make a *Ku Sung Thuk* offering[281] to Kyabjé Dodrupchen Rinpoche. I had prepared this offering since 2016 but never found the opportunity to present it.

During the *Ku Sung Thuk* offering, I felt entirely peaceful and at ease in the presence of a living Guru Rinpoche. During the offering, I made sincere prayers that may all sentient beings develop complete faith and devotion in their gurus and may all have similar opportunities to accumulate merits.

The compassion of my guru was all-pervading. After I walked back to my hotel room, I felt all my negative karma and inflicting emotions removed and a heavy burden taken off from my shoulders. This feeling lingered for some time. These were the direct and consequential blessings of the guru. Thus supplicating everything to your guru with complete faith and devotion is an effective method to receive blessings.

---

[280] Drubwang Penor Rinpoche, 2017, p. 91.

[281] *Ku Sung Thuk* offering is a symbolic offering of the enlightened body, speech, and mind of Buddha. The offering includes a Guru Rinpoche statue, Mandala, Stupa, and *Pecha*.

Figure 27. Receiving boundless blessings from the Great Dodrupchen Rinpoche during the *Ku Sung Thuk* offering.

My father was a genuine path-dweller in the Guru Yoga practice. He had developed almost a blind faith and devotion to his masters. Even to his last breath, he always dedicated everything to his gurus. I remember him telling me on many occasions, "Son, it is important to find a genuine, realised Dzogchen master. You should develop faith, devotion to even jumping off a cliff if your guru instructs you." Faith should not be misunderstood as an example of misuse of power by a teacher, preferably a skillful means to help students realize wisdom. These words have left an indelible mark on my life. It is the blessing of my father's prayers.

Lord Buddha summarised the merits of taking refuge in the

Three Jewels: "Even if someone could magically erect a stupa the size of the entire world and make vast, miraculous offerings to it for eons, the merit gained thereby would not constitute even a fraction of the merit gained by those who take refuge in the Three Jewels."[282]

Blessings of Mantras

I start this section by defining the word mantra and identifying why mantra recitation is a popular method amongst many practitioners and laypeople.

The word mantra combines the notions of ease and swiftness.[283] It protects our minds from negative thoughts. The recitation of the mantra is a popular method used by many Tibetan practitioners and laypeople.

The recitation of a mantra can help restore mental stability in moments of distress, doubt, nervousness, and fear. I recite the Guru Rinpoche mantra "OM AH HUM VAJRA GURU PADMA SIDDHI HUM." Amazingly, the negative emotions are immediately removed, and the feeling of safety and security prevail. I believe the mantra has spiritual power because it vibrates the truth and Buddhas' blessings.

When chanting a mantra, it energizes your breath that works directly on your mind and subtle body.[284] It constitutes a form of vipaśyanā [285] meditation. The essence of vipaśyanā realizes the real insights of things. Sitting straight in a cross-legged position in mediation is as much a ritualistic method as reciting mantra—both aim to seek the truth, to protect from negative thoughts, and to help us through difficulties.

---

[282] 84000: Translating the Words of the Buddha (2020).

[283] Dudjom Rinpoche, 2003, p. 9.

[284] Sogyal Rinpoche, 1994, p. 71.

[285] Vipaśyanā (Skt.; Tib. *Lhakthong*; Wyl. *lhag mthong*) is a meditation method of realising the truth.

During mantra recitation, you are not accumulating any negative karma of speech of slandering, lying, cheating, or toxic gossipping— already tremendous merit.

Just before her death, my late mother bought a Bodhi mālā that she could not use much. She often said, "Bodhi mālā is very good for reciting Guru Rinpoche's mantra." Knowingly or unknowingly, she bought it for me. After her death, I continue to recite the "Seven-Line Prayers" with her rosary, fulfilling her wish. I pray that all the merits accumulated will continue to guide all the sentient beings on the path to liberation in their present and future lives.

I find the matra recitation method a practical and effective one because of its simplicity. No elaborate ritualistic ceremonies are required. No specific location is needed. No particular time is needed. No significant investment is necessary. You just need a mālā and to dedicate time and recite daily—a perfect method for busy professionals, isn't it? People will accumulate tremendous merit if they recite a mantra with complete devotion and faith. Even reciting while watching YouTube, Facebook, Instagram will collect merits!

Figure 28. The Bodhi mālā of my late mother.

The Great Mipham Rinpoche explained that if we strive in the recitation of the "Seven-Line Prayer" with single-minded devotion and without distraction, this constitutes the approach phase; that when we begin to feel the effect of Guru Rinpoche's blessings, this is the close approach; that when signs of realization in waking life, in meditation, or in dreams, this is the accomplishment phase; that, finally, when we realize that the Guru and our minds are inseparable, this the great accomplishment.[286] Polu Khen Rinpoche used the blessings of a mantra to bring my father closer to the truth.

My father said:

"After many years of following and practicing, I went for a blessing audience with Polu Khen Rinpoche in Rajpur.[287] Due to impoverished conditions, like many other Tibetan refugees, Polu Khen Rinpoche resided like a renunciant Hindu Sadhu in an old house near a Hindu Mandir[288] located on a small hilltop. Many visitors—mainly worshippers—came to receive blessings. I requested for pith instructions in Dzogchen. Polu Khen Rinpoche told me to lay down on my back for a few hours on the top of a concrete water tank and asked me to look into the sky. I did exactly as instructed. But I didn't realize anything even after trying for hours. Out of dejection, I went to his presence again and told him that I had no realization whatsoever. Polu Khen Rinpoche realized that the prescribed method had not worked and asked me to go down the hill and recite twenty-one times *Sampa*

---

[286] Padmakar Translation Group, 2007, p. 36.

[287] Rajpur is a small town in Dehra Dun district in Uttarakhand, India. It is located on the Himalayan foothill of a popular hill station Mussoorie.

[288] Mandir means a Hindu temple in Hindi.

Lhundrupma. [289] Once again, I started reciting the mantra with great devotion and faith. When reaching halfway, a thought arose in my mind. I contemplated this thought for a while. At that moment, I realized that I can now go back to Polu Khen Rinpoche for further guidance and instructions. All the way through, I realized that Polu Khen Rinpoche was directing me to that thought. This is how I received the pith instructions from Polu Khen Rinpoche and how he became my root guru."

In the Great Perfection teachings, the relationship between a master and disciple is very sacred and secret, particularly all the pith instructions. Therefore, my father never shared what that "thought" was. In retrospect, I can only surmise that it must be related to the nature of the mind. I pray that may you also achieve realization through Buddhist mantras.

Recitation of Aspirational Prayers

Most of us have defilements and attachments that hinder us from becoming serious and diligent practitioners. Only a few can embark on the right path of realization. But we don't need to be discouraged, as all of us can be inspired by reciting aspiration prayers with enthusiasm and zeal. These prayers have blessings and compassion from the Buddhas and great masters.

In *The King of Aspiration Prayers: Samantabhadra's "Aspiration*

[289] *Sampa Lhundrupma* is a prayer to Guru Rinpoche that spontaneously fulfills all wishes. Lotsawa House, n.d. Free download at https://www.lotsawahouse.org/ tibetan-masters/chokgyur-dechen-lingpa/sampa-lhundrupma.

to Good Actions,"[290] there are prayers for purifying the mind, actual aspiration, extent of the aspiration, benefits of making aspirations, the dedication of the merits of this admirable aspiration, and conclusion. These prayers are not only virtuous but also vast and offer motivation and confidence in our practice.

The King of Aspiration Prayers encourages us to recite aspiration prayers to aspire to the grandest aspiration liberating all the sentient beings from suffering.

Daily Meditation

Meditation is an essential method of putting teachings into practice. These days the word "meditation" is so loosely used that its profound Buddhist meaning is not getting adequate attention. Many associate it with a meditation retreat at a sea-side hotel, although that might bring some temporary physical relaxation.

But the ultimate goal of mediation in Buddhism is to realize wisdom. Its method purifies our deluded minds and exhausts our habits, ultimately recognizing the true nature of our minds. In essence, meditation is a practice of getting used to our awareness by making it a part of our daily lives.

It's insufficient to only recognize the face of *rigpa*, the true nature of awareness in *Dzogpa Chenpo*. Recognizing it becomes the basis for further getting accustomed to it. A realised master can only introduce this awareness to a practitioner. The master who has gone through the path already. The only way to realize salt taste is

---

[290] Rigpa Shedra, 1996. The King of Aspiration Prayers: *Samantabhadra's "Aspiration to Good Actions"* (Skt. Ārya-Bhadracaryā-Praṇidhāna-Rāja; Tib. *Zangchö Mönlam*; Wyl. *bzang spyod smon lam*) is from the Gandavyūha chapter in Avatamsaka sūtra. You can download the complete transcript of the aspiration prayers from https://www.lotsawahouse.org/words-of-the-buddha/samantabhadra-aspiration-good-actions

by taking a pinch of it, though describing it in words can only help to understand its taste academically. Because there will be many ups and downs in the journey when you will need the wisdom of an experienced teacher for guidance and support navigating the tricky terrain of thoughts before reaching a high level of realization and stability in meditation.

A practitioner must continuously meditate to preserve the state of awareness. In this context, meditation means becoming familiar with the state of awareness, divested of all distraction and clinging.[291]

In a formal meditation session, Omniscient Longchenpa instructs a practitioner to sit on a wide seat straight and comfortably with the attitude of benefitting all living beings.[292] Don't follow after the past thoughts, don't bring forth future thoughts, and release the present sense from thinking.[293] Contemplate in the unwavering state without projections and withdrawals.[294] Remain in clarity, directness, and vividness in the union of emptiness and clarity; it realizes the Buddhas of the three times, the intrinsic nature of mind as it is; freedom from thoughts, analysis, and conceptualizations is the vision of the Buddhas.[295] Watch the ultimate peace of the inherent nature of mind; conclude the meditation session by dedicating the merits to all sentient beings.[296]

Great Dudjom Rinpoche offers further clarification, "... we can see that our present thoughts are just like waves on the water. At one moment, they arise; at another, they dissolve. And that's all there

[291] Dudjom Rinpoche, 2003, p. 86.

[292] Longchen Rabjam, 2002, p. 172. It is recommended to receive proper guidance and instructions from a realised master to mediate in this method prescribed by Omniscient Longchenpa.

[293] Longchen Rabjam, 2002, p. 172.

[294] Longchen Rabjam, 2002, p. 172.

[295] Longchen Rabjam, 2002, p. 172.

[296] Longchen Rabjam, 2002, p. 172.

is to it: the mind is nothing but thoughts. ... It is the mind itself that fabricates saṃsāra, and it does so because it fails to recognize its own nature. ...At the outset, thoughts appear and disappear in endless continuity. ... We must recognize thoughts as they arise."[297]

Additionally, Dudjom Rinpoche shared words of encouragement to those who are struggling in their meditation sessions, "Some people have lots of thoughts when they meditate—an unstoppable flood. If this happens to you, don't get upset and think that your meditation is a failure. It is a sign that you are becoming aware of the thoughts that, under ordinary circumstances, pass unnoticed."[298]

A few more words of advice. It is crucial to sit in the proper posture because within our body, there are many channels, and the heart channel and eye channel are connected.[299] Some meditate with closed eyes, and some with open eyes. The chances of falling asleep are higher with closed eyes. In Dzogchen mediation, the practitioner practices with their eyes open gazing at the tip of one's nose.

In the Guru Yoga practice, visualizing that your glorious master or Guru Rinpoche sitting one cubit above the crown of your head; that the master or Guru Rinpoche is the embodiment of all the Buddha; that the master or Guru Rinpoche dissolves into you; that your mind mingles with the mind of your master or Guru Rinpoche; and then rests in the natural state.[300] It is recommended that practitioners receive necessary empowerments before engaging in Vajrayāna meditations to receive the blessings of the lineage. Every practice has its own sets of empowerments and meditation methods.

You should be mindful of your awareness during meditation

---

[297] Dudjom Rinpoche, 2003, pp. 21-23.

[298] Dudjom Rinpoche, 2003, pp. 23-24.

[299] Drubwang Penor Rinpoche, 2017, p. 102.

[300] Drubwang Penor Rinpoche, 2017, p. 103.

and afterward when you are walking, eating, sitting, or sleeping.[301] The post-meditation is as crucial as during the meditation session. When going about the daily chores, a person should not allow the mind to be distracted by continuous streams of thoughts—instead, maintain awareness of them. One method is to visualize your guru or Guru Rinpoche sitting above the crown of your head all the time; while eating, visualize your guru or Guru Rinpoche residing at your throat; when going to sleep at night, visualize your master or Guru Rinpoche descending from your crown and resting in your heart center; while sleeping, engage in the Luminosity Yoga[302] giving you sound, peaceful sleep without bad dreams and transforming sleep into luminosity.[303]

These are useful and practical methods. If you could do a meditation session in the morning before starting your busy daily schedule, it can help to maintain better awareness throughout the day. Another practical, useful method for working professionals is to allocate a few minutes in a day to remind yourself of the passing distracting thoughts—keeping the amber of alertness. Reminding helps.

It's essential to measure the progress in your meditation. A practitioner has to be alert at all times. Dudjom Rinpoche advised that when a practitioner experiences wonder and bliss during meditation, it can be a useful landmark and could be a trap. If an attachment is developed—one should go beyond these experiences.[304] The snags can exhibit in many forms. For example, a blissful experience in meditation tricks you into believing that you have achieved a higher realization. This thought leads to self-pride which further gives rise

---

[301] Dudjom Rinpoche, 2003, p. 87.

[302] The Luminosity Yoga (Tib. *od* gsal; Skt. prabhāsvara) is a sleep yoga in Vajrayāna.

[303] Drubwang Penor Rinpoche, 2017, pp. 104-105.

[304] Sogyal Rinpoche, 1994, p. 45.

to arrogance. Here, a realized master can detect such traps and offer appropriate remedies. The safest barometer is when your devotion to your guru deepens and your compassion for sentient beings gains strength.[305]

It is vital to get used to meditation while disturbing things go on around you: it will help your mind meditate during *Bardo* when there are many frightening sounds and noises.[306] At the final moment of death, it would be excellent to control your mind and realize that death is just another thought that is giving an impression of dying.[307] Then the fear of death will subside like a child waking up from a nightmare.

Guru Rinpoche wonderfully summed up, "A hundred things may be explained, a thousand told, But one thing only should you grasp. Know one thing, and everything is freed—Remain within your inner nature, your awareness!"[308] Indeed, it is difficult to abide in the awareness of thoughts but with continuous efforts and perseverance, you will achieve a stable mind and relax in this state. May the blessings of all the Buddha accompany your practice.

Retire Early to Practice

Consider carefully your opportunities for Retiring Early to Practice. The ideal is combine the busy schedule and shortage of time of professional life with Buddhist practice. If this has not proved possible when you were younger, you can plan serious practice after retirement. Retirement ages vary between and within countries, 65 being not untypical. In the post-retirement years, you will perhaps

[305] Dudjom Rinpoche, 2003, p. 24.
[306] Drubwang Penor Rinpoche, 2017, p. 109.
[307] Dudjom Rinpoche, 2003, p. 24.
[308] Dudjom Rinpoche, 2003, p. 87.

spent a substantial part of your time going to doctors and hospitals. Your body might not support you physically, even when you are strong mentally. Is there any solution to this dilemma?

Yes, FIRE (Financial Freedom, Retire Early): maximising your investment growth over time through reduced spending, greater earnings, and wise investment.[309]

This is an increasingly popular concept that has evolved in recent years to retire early and enjoy the remaining life. Many aim for FIRE to enjoy life in pursuit of their passion: some traveling around the world, others spend more time on their hobbies, and many simply relax without the stress from work.

This concept can also open up an exciting option for path-seekers and path-dwellers. They can spend the remaining years of their lives on diligent and disciplined practice. In his later years, my father often advised me to consider early retirement and dedicate the remaining time to practice the Dharma. His words have always been lingering in my subconscious mind like a glowworm in a dark night. His words guided me to explore the FIRE concept.

The fundamentals of FIRE are:

- During your working career, one has to save enough to become financially independent in the later stages of a longer retirement.
- The total amount of savings should be enough to sustain your expenses without any income.
- The goal is to help you to lead a life of your deliberate choice.

This is a superficial summary but the concept is simple. Implementing these plans and achieving the goals is more challenging, requiring strict discipline and focus. You must make the initial decision to

---

[309] Prudential Investment Managers, 2018.

retire early. With this clarity of mind, you start to focus on planning for your FIRE strategy. It will be your execution that will determine your success:

- Make hay while the sun shines. Start saving money when you are earning money. In rudimentary financial jargon, save while your income is more than your expenses. It is for you to calculate your best balance between earning more or spending less.
- The habit of savings should start early in life when you decided to retire early. For example, your age now as you finish reading this book? Not to mean that your focus in life is only to save and retire early. Having fun, excitement, and exploration can go hand in hand throughout your life, but having a good life when you are young should not become an excuse not to save. The percentage of saving can be lower in your twenties or thirties than when you are in your forties or fifties. The essence is to have a disciplined saving habit from an early age.
- Long-term investment requires a learning curve. The selection of investment tools is plenty. The most common are stocks, ETFs (Exchange Traded Fund), real estate, gold, silver, oil, currencies, and so on. These investment options have varying levels of risks and return on investment. Take higher risks investments with higher returns, such as trading in stocks, when you are young early in your career, allowing for a higher capacity to take risks. As you mature and approach your retirement, reduce the risky investments in favor of Index ETFs with lower returns or a portfolio of both or real estate or funds. The records have shown that the Index ETFs (S&P 500, Dow Jones Industrial Average, Nasdaq

Composite, etc.) are a safe bet. Also consider investments in the property market. Investing in an apartment for rental. Your selection depends on your propensity for risk-taking and the returns you expect.

- Approaching the planned FIRE deadline, you should plan to invest in long-term investments with lower risks and lower returns. Taking unwarranted risks at this stage is not wise. An annual return on investment of 5-7% is a reasonable target. So a sound investment strategy is to have different investment portfolios at various stages of your life. When young, you can invest in higher risks and greater returns tools such as stocks. As you grow older, invest in less risky investments as Index ETFs.

- The essential FIRE calculation is to know how much you will need to live a decent life from your investments, your return on investment sustaining your living standard when you have no more regular income. Is it monthly US$ 1,000 or US$ 2,000 or US$ 5,000? Some people will opt to move to cheaper countries or locations within a country. For example, Swiss people might opt to move to Thailand to enjoy warm tropic weather at more affordable living costs. Your investments should provide the necessary amount to live your life happily after FIRE.

Besides leading a life of enjoyment and passion post-FIRE, I have suggested throughout this book "practice" as another attractive option for Buddhists. Without the stress of work, your mind will be more at ease and tranquility should help you settle down to practice with less distraction and deeper focus. Wise investments will provide additional security and peace of mind. I have thought seriously about FIRE and already started the journey towards achieving this goal.

Due to family obligations, it is hard to predict how soon I can achieve it. Nevertheless, I am targeting before sixty-five.

May all those who aim to FIRE and practice achieve their goals and become good path-dwellers!

Despite the worldly challenges, I decided to seek a path that allows me to combine a young family, busy profession, and Buddhist practice. I am happy to have looked within myself, taking my first step, and dedicating time and attention to my practice. If this is possible for me, I am sure you can do it too. Have confidence, faith, and devotion to the Buddha, Dharma, and Sangha. With some dedication and diligence, you can also progress in your path. Your frustration with the spiritual path is often an indication of you becoming a genuine Dharma practitioner.[310] Be optimistic, and start to seek a genuine guru, an excellent method is by reading *"The Words of My Perfect Teacher"* by the Great Master Patrul Rinpoche.

We learn about the Dharma through a guru and put the learning into practice through the Guru Yoga method. The most crucial goal of our practice is to tame our minds. The continuous introspection of our thoughts and slowly gaining constant awareness of the thoughts will lead to a stable mind and ultimately help us realize the true nature of the mind. The union of your faith and devotion with the blessings of your guru will surely lead you to a path of ultimate liberation. May all of you achieve liberation in this lifetime!

---

[310] Dzongsar Jamyang Khyentse, 2012, p. 46.

Epilogue

As long as space endures,
As long as there are sentient beings to be found,
May I continue likewise to remain
To drive away the sorrows of the world.[311]

Taking inspiration from the above famous quotation of great master Shāntideva, I hope you will make practice part of your life. My Epilogue is to help you with the decision to become a path-seeker. Seekers should target to realize the wisdom to find ultimate happiness in this life.

The book has pointed out that the benefits of practicing Dharma are not only for monks in monasteries but also for ordinary modern people. Practitioners should put the teachings of Buddha into action. Apply the union of methods and wisdom, using different methods according to your aptitudes and to find the truth.

The ultimate goal of a path-seeker is to achieve liberation, by realizing the wisdom, from the distractions of samsāra. These distractions keep us too busy to see the true nature of our minds and the projected world.

---

[311] Padmakara Translation Group, 2006, p. 171. This is the famous quote by Great Shāntideva (c.685-763), who was a great master, scholar, bodhisattva, and the author of the prominent Bodhicharyāvatāra.

There are too many trends for making people "feel" good, for only feeling good. It seems better to have a full-body massage or to listen to popular music than to practice the Dharma.[312] The sincere aspiration to practice Dharma is to attain liberation. Out of compassion and not to brandish realized wisdom, the teachings of Buddha Śākyamuni showed a path to liberation. This compassion was so profound and vast to say the unsayable, express the inexpressible and define the indefinable of the nature of truth.

In the view of *Dzogpa Chenpo*, all phenomena have always been pure, including our minds. All of our faults, defilements, and negative emotions are temporary. For this reason, we can be confident that all people really can become enlightened.[313] Like a car through a muddy road, although it is stained by dirty mud, we are totally confident of regaining its original gloss after a thorough carwash: the dirt is only a temporary phenomenon—not its true nature. The Great Dudjom Rinpoche beautifully summarized: "The root of Dharma is your mind. Tame it and you're practicing the Dharma. To practice Dharma is to tame your mind—And when you tame it, then you will be free!"[314]

84,000 paths can help you to bring you closer to wisdom. The distraction of busy lifestyles—filled with appointments, watching movies, chatting on instant messaging apps, playing video games, going shopping, and work—takes you away from following a path. But if you could squeeze in a few minutes and dedicate them to your daily practice, it will offer you a chance to progress in your path. Initially difficult but persistence will help to turn this into a new

---

[312] Dzongsar Jamyang Khyentse, 2012, p. 5.

[313] 84000: Translating the Words of the Buddha, 2017, p.33.

[314] Dudjom Rinpoche, 2003, p. 29.

habit. As Guru Rinpoche said, "My view is higher than the sky, but my attention to actions and their results is finer than flour."[315]

Choose your most suitable methods as a path-seeker, and continue practicing with greater mindfulness by combining methods to realize the wisdom. Let me list the methods mentioned in the five chapters with opportunities for combination—and many more to be explored during your seeking:

1. Observing the phenomenon of "Samsāra and Śūnyatā" (Chapter 1).
2. Understanding "The Four Truths" (Chapter 1).
3. Seeking a "genuine Guru" (Chapter 1).
4. Remembering the "blessings of your Guru" (Chapter 1).
5. Believing in "Karma: causes, conditions, and results" (Chapter 1-5).
6. Realizing the "Buddhist Paths = Methods + Wisdom" (Chapter 2).
7. Reciting and realizing the "Prajna Paramita Sūtra" (Chapter 2).
8. Remembering "Guru Rinpoche" (Chapter 1-5).
9. Understanding and realizing "Dzogpa Chenpo" (Chapter 1-5).
10. Going to "Pilgrimage" to holy Buddhist sites (Chapter 2).
11. Paying attention to your "shift" as a seeker (Chapter 3).
12. Taking "refuge in Buddha, Dharma, and Sangha" (Chapter 1-5).
13. Gaining guidance from your Guru (Chapter 1-5).
14. Practicing the path of the "Seven-Line Prayer" (Chapter 3).
15. Practicing "diligence" in your practice (Chapter 1-5).
16. Trusting in "treasure teachings" (Chapter 4).

---

[315] Dudjom Rinpocher, 2003, p. 88.

17. Practicing the "teachings of Khandro Yeshé Tsogyal" (Chapter 4).

18. Practicing the "teachings of Sera Khando" (Chapter 4).

19. Practicing the "teachings of Kandro Tāre Lhamo" (Chapter 4).

20. Reciting "The Tibetan Book of the Dead (Bardo Thödol)" (Chapter 4).

21. Practicing "The Tibetan Book of the Dead (Bardo Thödol)" (Chapter 4).

22. Doing "*Zhitro*" pūjās (Chapter 4).

23. Living and dying "consciously" (Chapter 4).

24. Practicing the path of "faith and devotion" (Chapter 5).

25. Reciting and realizing the "Vimalakīrti Sūtra" (Chapter 5).

26. Examing the "dualistic mind" (Chapter 5).

27. Practicing "Guru Yoga" (Chapter 5).

28. Practicing "accumulation of merits" (Chapter 5).

29. Practicing "mantra recitation" (Chapter 5).

30. Practicing "daily meditation" (Chapter 5).

The path-seekers should choose methods they feel most likely to follow and without worrying about the others. All depends on individual habits and preferences. Some people might find reciting mantra easy to apply or others might prefer offering flowers to the Buddha or many might like lighting of butter lamps in the monasteries or might desire to carve mantras on rocks or hoist prayer flags in their gardens, while countless people are attracted to meditation.

I would advise the readers to base their selection decision on two criteria: (1) which methods strike you most forcibly, and which have the strongest spiritual meaning and impact to you—whether off the top of the head or by reading them back again from earlier in the chapters; and (2) how well each fits into your life as it is or as you will be leading it. Every method is individual, but the ultimate goal is the same—to realize the wisdom.

On the path-seeking journey, meaningful progress consists of big long-term spiritual benefits but also short-term worldly benefits. Here I would like to share the achievable interesting worldly benefits that come as an additional bonus.

The first benefit in my case is that the intensity of "greed" has weakened in a good way. I am not massaging my greed for material gains—not a nihilistic approach to negating material gains. I need to make more money but only as much as necessary, and through fair and honest methods and without tarnishing my Buddhist beliefs. With additional spare income, we can help more people in need and donate more money to non-profit organizations.

The second benefit is that I find it easier to offer "generosity" to the needy. More willing and open to donations, sponsorship and financial help to the poor. Unlike in the past, the scope of generosity is more broad-based than to close family members or relatives or friends. Also, at work, I am more able and willing to offer help and guidance to my colleagues and customers without expectation.

The third benefit is that the outburst of "emotions" are better under control. The anger still arrives with its vengeance, but it subsides in a shorter period than before. Instead of anger taking over the reins, I have more control over it than vice versa. This helps to keep away big quarrels from the dining table and offers a conducive environment for a civilized dialog on emotional and sensitive topics.

The fourth benefit is that I have developed an "accommodating" attitude. Yangchen experienced that I was more willing to listen to a different opinion or point-of-view from her and Tsering. Becoming more accommodating when there is an outburst of anger from others. Not stopping family members from developing their own space and freedom.

The fifth benefit is that the "easygoing" approach towards life. There are bound to be many crises in life, whether self-inflicted or not. One approach is to take each of them seriously but a smarter way is to be more relaxed. More often than not, taking seriously blows the issue out of control. Usually, a composed approach towards a crisis is a simple and direct method of resolving it. For example, we have some issues with our seventeen-year-old son. We let time run its course and readdress them in the future, making our lives more peaceful.

The sixth benefit is that I can adapt to changes at work more comfortably. Companies use "change" strategies to improve productivity and profits. Many find drastic changes challenging to adapt to, ultimately leading to disappointment, frustration, and quitting. A composed and open-minded approach to this reduces my mental stress and leads to more harmony in the family.

The seventh benefit is that we can teach our son to respect his teachers. For example, we often quote an ancient Indian tradition of Guru-Shishya Parampara: guru means a teacher, shishya means a student, and parampara means a tradition. The relationship between a teacher and a student is sacred and lifelong in this tradition—the student's reverence and devotion to the teacher are at the same level as a spiritual guru, and love and kindness from the teacher are like parents to their children. Even today, this tradition is still witnessed in India, for example, in classical Indian music and dance.

Based on this wonderful ancient Indian tradition, we have been teaching Tsering that his first teacher is his parents, who taught him how to walk and speak, protected him from illness, introduced the workings of this world, taught him morality, shared the teachings of the Buddha, and introduced him to great Buddhist masters, and so on.

The next are the school teachers who teach him how to read

and write and give him all the knowledge that he will require in the future, and the motivation to continue learning; therefore, he should offer his respect and appreciation to them for imparting such valuable knowledge. But not all teachers should take respect from students for granted—they are not entitled to but must earn it. Those lazy and incompetent teachers must be subjected to scrutiny and criticism to improve their teachings skills. Instead of thinking that the teachers are paid to teach, Tsering should appreciate the opportunity to learn and thank the teacher who brings this learning to him. Appreciation of teachers will help him to learn how to appreciate other things in life too.

Teachers expect respect from students but also need to learn how to provide love and kindness for students to expect. This is a selection matter before it is a training need. Screen out in the selection process those teacher applicants who cannot be taught how to teach with love and kindness. Rely less on qualification and look more deeply into motivation and personality because teaching is always two-way communication and relationship.

Before starting this journey to seek the truth, first, one must decide to be a path-seeker and then with a clear mind, plan and organize to begin the search. Where to start?

Before you can set out on your Buddhist path, you have to find it; before you can find it, you have to search; but before you explore, you need to decide that this is definitely what you are going to do and what you want: make up your mind first about becoming a path-seeker and then seek. This will be a big decision, as spiritual and emotional as the path itself, a commitment to seek systematically and calmly.

You can't search for your path while still considering and worrying about whether you should or whether this is what you want to do. You can't wholeheartedly plunge into path-seeking while hesitating whether to take the plunge in the first place. To quit smoking, we have to decide and convince ourselves to stop smoking and stop worrying, stop delaying, stop experimenting with alternative products. It is impossible to give up until we have decided and know the decision is taken. Choose your method, and taking the first step will be easier and smoother. The decision to seek clears your mind to move forward on path-seeking in a new positive and determined frame of mind.

Perhaps you can decide right now; or you need more time to ponder over; or let the book sink in more deeply and firmly—then decide. Set yourself a fixed date for your decision, for example, changing jobs or employers. Do not prevaricate and risk missing the now-or-never moment, possibly losing the opportunity forever. Systematically plan rather than wasting your time. You might have already decided: Congratulations, now choose your methods.

Taking big decisions in life eliminates a lot of little decisions thereafter. Once you have decided to be a path-seeker, you don't have to hesitate daily about whether you can find time to meditate or recite mantras or recite aspirational prayers. You have already decided therefore fully committed.

Let me share a touching poem from Kyabjé Nyoshul Khenpo Jamyang Dorje[316] (1932-1999), a highly realized Tibetan *Dzogpa Chenpo* meditation master. He composed a lovely poem *Natural Great Peace*[317] that describes how a practitioner should rest in the natural state of mind:

> "Rest in natural great peace
> This exhausted mind
> Beaten helplessly by karma and neurotic thoughts

---

[316] Popularly known as Nyoshul Khen Rinpoche.
[317] Tib. *rang bzhin zhi ba chen po.*

Like the relentless fury of pounding waves
In the infinite ocean of samsāra." [318]

I pray that all of you can find this natural great peace in your practice and be able to sustain it throughout the remaining years of your lives. I hope to publish my aspirational prayers to all modern Buddhist path-seekers: May you take the first step to seek a Buddhist path; May you find a genuine Buddhist master who is only interested in your awakening; May you develop an untainted, pure perception of your guru under all circumstances without preconditions; May you firmly rest in the castle of śūnyatā; and, ultimately, may you overcome distractions and duality to go beyond meditation in this lifetime.

---

[318] Lotsawa House, n.d., *Natural Great Peace*. Click here https://www.youtube.com/ watch?v=Gvo-CCtC3Zs to listen to the poem in a soothing melody.

Bibliography

84000: Translating the Words of the Buddha (2017). *The Sūtra of The Teaching of Vimalakīrti*. Retrieved from http://84000.co/doc/ vimalakirti/Vimalakirti%20Book_E_screen-170724.pdf

84000: Translating the Words of the Buddha (2020). *Taking Refuge in the Three Jewels: Triśaraṇagamana*. Retrieved from https:// read.84000.co/translation/toh225.html

Chatral Rinpoche (2007). *Compassionate Action*. (Larson, Z., Ed.). Boulder: Snow Lion Publications.

Chönyi Drolma (2017, Trans.). *The Life and Visions of Yeshé Tsogyal: The Autobiography of the Great Wisdom Queen*. (A Treasure Text Discovered by Drimé Kunga). Boulder: Snow Lion. (Original work published in 14th century).

Dilgo Khyentse (2007). Padmakara Translation Group. (2007). *The Heart of Compassion: The Thirty Seven Verses on the Practise of a Bodhisattva*. (Padmakara Translation Group, Trans.). Boston: Shambhala Publications.

Drubwang Penor Rinpoche (2017). *An Ocean of Blessings: Heart Teachings of Drubwang Penor Rinpoche*. (Ani Jinba Palmo, Trans. and Tweed, M. Eds.). Boulder: Snow Lion.

Dudjom Rinpoche (1979, May). *Dudjom Rinpoche about Meditation 1979* [Video Podcast]. Retrieved from https://www.youtube.com/watch?v=qbJ7u_nJb54

Dudjom Rinpoche, Jikdrel Yeshe Dorje (1991). *The Nyingma School of Tibetan Buddhism, Its Fundamentals and History*. (Gyurme Dorje & M. Kapstein, Trans. & Eds.). Boston: Wisdom Publications. (Original work was published in Tibetan).

Dudjom Rinpoche (2003). *Counsels from My Heart*. (Padmakara Translation Group, Trans.). Boston: Shambhala Publications.

Dudjom Rinpoche, Sangye Pema Shepa (2019, April 19). *A Brief History of the Troma Nagmo practice from the Dudjom Lineage*. Retrieved from http://www.dunzhuxinbaozang.com/newsitem/278274501

Dzongsar Jamyang Khyentse (2007). *What Makes You Not a Buddhist*. New Delhi: Timeless Books.

Dzongsar Jamyang Khyentse (2011a, September 8). *Dzongsar Khyentse's 宗薩欽哲 teaching on Bardo 中陰 Part 1 of 31* [Video Podcast]. Retrieved from https://www.youtube.com/watch?v=XTyishDMyF0

Dzongsar Jamyang Khyentse (2011b, September 10). *BARDO 中陰 Teaching by Dzongsar Khyentse Rinpoche 宗萨钦哲仁波切*

10 [Video Podcast]. Retrieved from https://www.youtube.com/ watch?v=hra48x5PRJw&t=21s

Dzongsar Jamyang Khyentse (2011c, September 10). *BARDO* 中 *阴 Teaching by Dzongsar Khyentse Rinpoche 宗萨钦哲仁波切 -11* [Video Podcast]. Retrieved from https://www.youtube.com/ watch?v=z1wzACaso-k

Dzongsar Jamyang Khyentse (2011d, September 10). *BARDO* 中 *阴 Teaching by Dzongsar Khyentse Rinpoche 宗萨钦哲仁波切 - 12* [Video Podcast]. Retrieved from https://www.youtube.com/ watch?v=MAbEwGeQxCw

Dzongsar Jamyang Khyentse (2011e, September 10). *BARDO* 中 *阴 Teaching by Dzongsar Khyentse Rinpoche 宗萨钦哲仁波切 -13* [Video Podcast]. Retrieved from https://www.youtube.com/ watch?v=yladxfn_0jk

Dzongsar Jamyang Khyentse (2011f, September 10). *BARDO* 中 *阴 Teaching by Dzongsar Khyentse Rinpoche 宗萨钦哲仁波 切 – 14* [Video Podcast]. Retrieved from https://www.youtube.com/ watch?v=6kLT0rBWLVA

Dzongsar Jamyang Khyentse (2011g, September 10). *BARDO* 中 *阴 Teaching by Dzongsar Khyentse Rinpoche 宗萨钦哲仁波 切 – 15* [Video Podcast]. Retrieved from https://www.youtube.com/ watch?v=VyJ55EgJpEo

Dzongsar Jamyang Khyentse (2011h, September 13). *BARDO* 中 *阴 Teaching by Dzongsar Khyentse Rinpoche 宗萨钦哲仁波 切 – 16* [Video Podcast]. Retrieved from https://www.youtube.com/ watch?v=iDa3b2Z2U-Q

Dzongsar Jamyang Khyentse (2011i, September 13). *BARDO* 中 阴 *Teaching by Dzongsar Khyentse Rinpoche* 宗萨钦哲仁波 切 *– 17* [Video Podcast]. Retrieved from https://www.youtube.com/ watch?v=5RjVoK7L_tM

Dzongsar Jamyang Khyentse (2011j, September 13). *BARDO* 中 阴 *Teaching by Dzongsar Khyentse Rinpoche* 宗萨钦哲仁波 切 *– 18* [Video Podcast]. Retrieved from https://www.youtube.com/ watch?v=nPoMB9_X1uM

Dzongsar Jamyang Khyentse (2011k, September 14). *BARDO* 中 阴 *Teaching by Dzongsar Khyentse Rinpoche* 宗萨钦哲仁波 切 *– 19* [Video Podcast]. Retrieved from https://www.youtube.com/ watch?v=-KgC4g48Odo

Dzongsar Jamyang Khyentse (2011l, September 14). *BARDO* 中 阴 *Teaching by Dzongsar Khyentse Rinpoche* 宗萨钦哲仁波 切 *– 20* [Video Podcast]. Retrieved from https://www.youtube.com/ watch?v=anieyzueiQM

Dzongsar Jamyang Khyentse (2011m, September 14). *Bardo 21 Teaching by Dzongsar Khyentse Rinpoche* 宗萨钦哲仁波 切 *– 21* [Video Podcast]. Retrieved from https://www.youtube.com/ watch?v=RfxqP9tTVk4

Dzongsar Jamyang Khyentse (2012). *Not for Happiness: A Guide to the So-Called Preliminary Practices.* Boston: Shambhala South Asia Editions.

Dzongsar Jamyang Khyentse (2016). *The Guru Drinks Bourbon.* (Ben-Yehuda, A., Ed.). Boulder: Shambhala Publications.

Dzongsar Jamyang Khentse (2018a, February 26). *Dzongsar Khyentse Rinpoche ~ Vajrayana Buddhism in the Modern World, Berlin Talk* [Video Podcast]. Retrieved from https://www.youtube.com/watch?v=NWcjJzmOKQk

Dzongsar Jamyang Khentse (2018b). *LIVING IS DYING: How to Prepare for Dying, Death and Beyond.* Retrieved from https://www.siddharthasintent.org/assets/Global-Files/Publications/LivingisDyingEdition3.pdf under a Creative Commons CC BY-NC-ND (Attribution-Non-commercial-No-derivatives) 3.0 copyright https://creativecommons.org/licenses/by-nc-nd/4.0/

Erik Pema Kunsang (1999, Trans.) *Dakini Teachings: Padmasambhavas Oral Instructions to Lady Tsogyal.* (Recorded and concealed by Yeshe Tsogyal and revealed by Nyang Ral Nyingma Öser and Sangye Lingpa. Translated according the oral teachings by Kyabjé Tulku Urgyen Rinpoche). Boudhanath: Rangjung Yeshe Publications.

Fremantle, F. & Chögyam Trungpa (Eds.). (1987). *The Tibetan Book of the Dead: The Great Liberation Through Hearing in the Bardo.* Boston: Shambala Publication.

Gayley, H. (2017). *Love Letters from Golok: A Tantric Couple in Modern Tibet.* New York: Columbia University Press.

Jacoby, Sarah H. (2016). *Love and Liberation: Autobiographical Writings of the Tibetan Buddhist Visionary Sera Khandro.* New York: Columbia University Press.

Karma Lingpa (n.d.). *The Peaceful and Wrathful Deities. The Profound Dharma of Self-liberated Wisdom Mind: the Great*

Liberation through Hearing in the Bardo (Tib. *zab chos zhi khro dgongs pa rang grol: bar do thos grol chen mo*). Majnukatilla, Delhi: Chosspyod Publication.

Kwan Um School of Zen (n.d.). *The Maha Prajna Paramita Hrdaya Sutra*. Retrieved May 30, 2019, from https://static1.squarespace. com/static/58d013bbe58c6272b30dad0b/t/59b04a9fd55b41f0f3 33b554/1504725663797/Heart-Sutra-in-English-text1.pdf

Lāma Kazi Dawa-Samdup (2017). *The Tibetan Book of the Dead*. Available from https://www.amazon.com/gp/ product/B071RFF4RL?pf_rd_p=2d1ab404-3b11-4c97-b3db-48081e145e35&pf_rd_r=36QCJJFR09NHF3X60PGF

Longchen Rabjam (2002). *The Practice of Dzogchen*. (Tulku Thondup, Trans. and Talbott, H.,Eds.). New York: Snow Lion Publications.

Longchen Rabjampa Drime Wözer (n.d.). *The Four-Themed Precious Garland, An Introduction to Dzogchen, the Great Completeness* (*chos-bzhi rin-chen phreng-ba*). (Berzin, A., Sharpa Tulku, & Kapstein, M., Trans.). Dharamsala: The Library of Tibetan Works and Archives. (The translation was first published 1979).

Lotsawa House (n.d.). *Natural Great Peace*. Retrieved December 7, 2019, from https://www.lotsawahouse.org/tibetan-masters/ nyoshul-khenpo-jamyang-dorje/natural-great-peace

Lotsawa House (n.d.). *Sampa Lhundrupma: The Prayer to Guru Rinpoche that Spontaneously Fulfils all Wishes*. Retrieved July 20, 2020, from https://www.lotsawahouse.org/tibetan-masters/ chokgyur-dechen-lingpa/sampa-lhundrupma

Lotsawa House (n.d.). *The Excellent Path to Omniscience: The Dzogchen Preliminary Practice of Longchen Nyingtik.* Retrieved August 2, 2020, from https://www.lotsawahouse.org/tibetan-masters/dodrupchen-I/longchen-nyingtik

Lotsawa House (n.d.). *The Sūtra of the Heart of Transcendent Wisdom.* Retrieved July 3, 2020, from https://www.lotsawahouse.org/words-of-the-buddha/heart-sutra-with-extras

Nakamoto, S. (2009). *Bitcoin: A Peer-to-Peer Electronic Cash System.* Retrieved June 30, 2019, from https://bitcoin.org/bitcoin.pdf

Nyoshul Khenpo Jamyang Dorjé (2005). *A Marvelous Garland of Rare Gems: Biographies of Masters of Awareness in the Dzogchen Lineage. A Spiritual History of the Teachings of Natural Great Perfection.* . (Barron, R. (Chökyi Nyima, Trans.). Junction City: Padma Publishing.

Padmakara Translation Group (1998, Trans.). *The Words of My Perfect Teacher by Patrul Rinpoche.* Boston: Shambhala Publications. (Original work was published in Tibetan in Tibet).

Padmakara Translation Group (2006, Trans.). *The Way of The Bodhisattva (Bodhicharyāvatāra) by Shāntideva.* Boston: Shambhala Publications.

Padmakara Translation Group (2012, Trans.). *Lady of the Lotus-Born; The Life and Enlightenment of Yeshe Tsogyal.* (A Translation of The Lute Song of the Gandharvas, A Revelation in Eight Chapters of the Secret History of the Life and Enlightenment of Yeshe Tsogyal, Queen of Tibet, a Treasure text committed to writing by Gyalwa

Changchub and Namkhai Nyingpo, Discovered by Tertön Taksham Samten Lingpa). Boston: Shambhala Publications

Padmakara Translation Group (2016, Trans.). *White Lotus by Jamgön Mipham*. Boston: Shambhala Publications.

Prudential Investment Managers (2018). *How to retire early with FIRE*. Retrieved April 10, 2021, from https://www.prudential.co.za/media/30865/how-to-retire-early-with-fire.pdf

Rigpa Shedra (1996). *The King of Aspiration Prayers: Samantabhadra's "Aspiration to Good Actions" (Skt. Ārya-Bhadracaryā-Praṇidhāna-Rāja; Tib. Zangchö Mönlam; Wyl. bzang spyod smon lam)*. Retrieved December 8, 2019, from https://www.lotsawahouse.org/words-of-the-buddha/samantabhadra-aspiration-good-actions

Rigpa Shedra (2014). *Guru Yoga*. Retrieved July 15, 2020, from https://www.rigpawiki.org/index.php?title=Guru_Yoga

Rigpa Shedra (2017). *Eight Manifestations of Guru Rinpoche*. Retrieved November 26, 2019, from https://www.rigpawiki.org/index.php?title=Eight_Manifestations_of_Guru_Rinpoche

Rigpa Shedra (2018). *Dudjom Sangye Pema Shepa Rinpoche*. Retrieved October 27, 2019, from https://www.rigpawiki.org/index.php?title=Dudjom_Sangye_Pema_Shepa_Rinpoche

Rigpa Shedra (2019). *Padmasambhava*. Retrieved December 4, 2019, from https://www.rigpawiki.org/index.php?title=Padmasambhava

Sogyal Rinpoche (1994). *The Tibetan Book of Living and Dying.* (Gaffney, P. and Harvey, A., Eds.). New York: HarperCollins Publishers.

Taiwan Centers for Disease Control. (2020). *Coronavirus disease 2019 (COVID-19).* Retrieved November 21, 2020, from http:// https:// www.cdc.gov.tw/en

Tashi Gelek (2013). Compassion in Buddhism and Guanxi: Can There Be a Synergy for Western Companies in China. *Chinese Business Review, 12, 4,* 287-297.

Thinley Norbu (2004). *The Sole Panacea: A Brief Commentary on the Seven-Line Prayer to Guru Rinpoche That Cures the Suffering of the Sickness of Karma and Defilement.* Boston: Shambhala Publications.

Tourism Shikoku (2020). *What is the Shikoku pilgrimage?* Retrieved April 9, 2020, from https://shikoku-tourism.com/en/shikoku-henro/ shikoku-henro

Tulku Thondup (2002). *Masters of Meditation and Miracles: Lives of the Great Buddhist Masters of India and Tibet.* (Talbott, H., Ed.). Boston: Shambhala Publications.

Tulku Thondup Rinpoche (1997). *Hidden Teachings of Tibet: An Explanation of the Terma Tradition of Tibetan Buddhism.* (Talbott, H., Ed.). Boston: Wisdom Publications.

Wylie, Turrell V. (1959). A STANDARD OF TIBETAN TRANSCRIPTION. *Harvard Journal of Asiatic Studies,* 22, 261-267.

List of Illustrations

Information Panels

The information panels are additional explanations for non-Buddhist readers to understand Buddhist concepts or for everyone on general topics.

Figures

Tables

Transliteration of Tibetan Names

- In this book, I have used *italics* for all the Tibetan words, except for the people's names. The Tibetan names are used in the most common transliteration, for example, "Tashi" is used instead of *"bkra shis"* in the Wylie system of transliteration.

- I have used the Wylie transliteration system (Wyl.) for transcribing Tibetan into Roman script. In 1959, Professor Turrell V. Wylie—a scholar, Tibetologist, and sinologist—devised the Wylie transliteration system to transcribe Tibetan words into English. He developed a standard system of Tibetan transcription for uniformity in order to facilitate and standardize the advancement of Tibetan studies.[319] For example, the "Seven-Line Prayer" as *"tshig bdun gsol debs."*

- I have used Tib. to denote Tibetan words, e.g., *"gompa* (Tib., monastery)" means that it is a Tibetan word for monastery.

- Most Tibetans have two first names, often without a family name. For example, Tsering Yangchen. At times, individuals have a family name followed by a personal name: Shangritsang Tsering Yangchen or Tsering Yangchen Shangritsang. I have used first names for common Tibetan people.

- Kyabjé Polu Khen Rinpoche Dorje (also known as Thupten Kunga Gyaltsen but popularly known as Polu Khen Rinpoche)

---

[319] Wylie, 1959, p. 263.

is another example showing the complexity of Tibetan names. When mentioned for the first time, the full name or different names are mentioned but later used the most commonly known name in recurring situations.

- Vajrayāna is a Tantrayāna form of Buddhism in Tibet, Bhutan, and other Himalayan regions. I have used both words in the book.

- For *Dzogpa Chenpo*, we used other different names as well, for example, Dzogchen or Mahāsaṅdhi or Atiyoga or Great Perfection or Great Completeness.

- *Pemajungné* is also known as Guru Rinpoche (Precious Master) or Guru Padmasambhava or the lotus-born or *Pemajungné* (Tib.) in Tibet and other Himalayan regions. I have used these different names in the book.

- Avalokiteśvara has many different names in different languages, e.g., Avalokiteśvara in Sanskrit, *Chenrezig* in Tibetan, and Guanyin in Chinese. Symbolically, Avalokiteśvara is represented in male and female forms in Tibetan and Chinese Buddhist traditions.

- In Tibetan Buddhism, a Tulku means living Buddha or a reincarnated Lama, and Rinpoche means "precious gem," an honorific term not only for a Tulku but also for those lamas who hold highly esteemed positions in a monastery such as an abbot or highly realized masters.

- Kyabjé is a honorific title in Tibetan for the "Lord of Refuge." It is used for higly realised Buddhist masters. I have used this title for great Buddhist masters and often used synonyms such as Great or Renowned or Realized masters.

- In Tibetan Buddhism, there are many past incarnations of great masters. There are four incarnations of Kyabjé Dodrupchen Rinpoche hitherto. Unless mentioned explicitly, I have used

Dodrupchen Rinpoche as a short form for the Fourth Kyabjé Dodrupchen Rinpoche, Jigmé Tubten Trinlé Palbar.

- In Dudjom Lingpa's case, the reincarnation is Dudjom Rinpoche, Jikdrel Yeshe Dorje, and Dudjom Rinpoche, Sangye Pema Shepa is the reincarnation of his predecessor. For simplification, I have used Dudjom Rinpoche as Jikdrel Yeshe Dorjee and Dudjom Yangsi Rinpoche as Sangye Pema Shepa.

- The *Bardo Thödol* is initially written in Tibetan and translated as *The Tibetan Book of the Dead* in English. I have used both words in the book.

- Khandro will be used in italics for all the nouns except for proper nouns, for example, Khandro Yeshé Tsogyal, Sera Khandro, and Kandro Tāre Lhamo.

Glossary of Words

Asura: Demigod.

Avalokiteśvara (Skt.): The bodhisattva of compassion, also known as *Chenrezig* in Tibetan. The "Om Mani Padme Hum" mantra of *Chenrezig* is very popular in the Himalayan regions. The compassionate Avalokiteśvara has taken different forms to benefit the sentient beings: male in Tibetan *gompas* and female in Chinese temples.

Bardo: The intermittent period between death and birth. *The Tibetan Book of the Dead* (*Bardo Thödol*) explains *bardo* in great depth. Refer to Chapter 4 for more explanation.

Bodhichitta (Tib. *byang chub kyi sem*): It means the awakened state of mind. The wish to achieve Buddhahood for the sake of others through the practice of love and compassion. The deeper meaning is the direct realization of the ultimate nature of the mind.

Bodhisattvas (Skt.; Tib. *chang chub sempa*; **Wyl.** *byang chub sems dpa'*): Someone who practices the Bodhisattvas path with the ultimate goal to bring all sentient beings to enlightenment. It also means a sublime being who has attained one of ten stages of the Bodhisattva path.

Buddha Dharma: The teachings of the Buddha. It contains the transmission and the application of the teachings.

Buddha Śākyamuni: The Buddha of our time. Often referred to as Lord Buddha, and sometimes as Buddha.

Cham: It's an elaborate spiritual dance in Vajrayāna Buddhism.

Chatral Sangye Dorje Rinpoche (Chatral Rinpoche): One of the Great Tibetan masters of *Dzogpa Chenpo*. He was one of the gurus of the fifth Reting Rinpoche in Tibetan. He was known as Chatral Rinpoche, who has given up on worldly wealth and fame, and meditated for many decades as a wandering yogi in most of the Guru Rinpoche caves in Tibet, Bhutan, India, and Nepal. With unbiased love, kindness, and compassion, Chatral Rinpoche became the root guru of Dudjom Yangsi Rinpoche and bestowed all the profound Dzogchen empowerments and teachings for the future generations to benefit from the turning of the Dharma wheel by Dudjom Yangsi Rinpoche.

Dākinī (Skt.; Tib. *Khandro* or *Khandroma*): Non-gender specific, meaning someone who freely moves in the state of wakefulness. They are the guardians of Tantrayāna. In this book, we have given examples of female dākinī in Tibet. Refer to Chapter 4 for more details.

Derge: A region in eastern Tibet, Kham.

Dharma: See Buddha Dharma.

Dharmakāya: The śunyatā (emptiness) aspect of Buddhahood.

Dodrupchen Rinpoche, Jigmé Tubten Trinlé Palbar: A revered and highly realized living *Dzogpa Chenpo* master of our time. He is the living Guru Rinpoche in the flesh. Refer to Chapter 3 for more understanding of the Dodrupchen Lineage.

Dualism: This is an important subject in Buddhism. Simply, it is the grasping and subjective concept of "I" and "other." Our skeptic minds always judge what is right or wrong, good or bad, rich or poor, and so on. Continuous judgments give rise to dualism. The antidote to dualism is nondualism: wisdom when you go beyond subject and object. Refer to Chapter 5 for more details.

Dudjom Rinpoche, Jikdrel Yeshe Dorje: One of the most renowned and realized Tibetan Buddhist masters of the 20th century. He was the regent of Guru Rinpoche in our world. Kyabjé Dudjom Rinpoche was a prolific writer, poet, *Tertön*, and highly realized meditator master. He was the direct reincarnation of the Great Dudjom Lingpa. And revealed many *termas* and practices which are still followed by his disciples around the world. His disciples included many highly realized masters of our time including Chatral Rinpoche, Dilgo Khyentse Rinpoche, Tulku Urgyen Rinpoche, Dungsey Thinley Norbu Rinpoche, Dzongsar Jamyang Khyentse Rinpoche, and so on. His reincarnation is Dudjom Yangsi Rinpoche, Sangye Pema Shepa.

Dudjom Yangsi Rinpoche, Sangye Pema Shepa: He is the reincarnation of Dudjom Rinpoche, Jikdrel Yeshe Dorje. In Tibet, Kandro Tāre Lhamo recognized him based on a prophecy. Later acknowledged by many great Tibetan masters inside and outside Tibet. From his childhood, Kyabjé Chatral Rinpoche took care of him like a father and became his root guru. He has been tirelessly teaching the Dudjom Tersar teachings including Troma Nagmo around the world. In this book, I used Dudjom Yangsi Rinpoche as his name. Refer to Chapter 4 for more details.

Dzogchen or *Dzongpa Chenpo* (Tib; Wyl. *rdzogs pa chen po*; Skt. Mahāsaṅdhi or Atiyoga): "Dzogpa" means complete or the end, and "chenpo" means great. In English, widely translated as Great

Perfection or Great Completeness. It is the ground, path, and fruition. The ground is that we are already in a state of the self-perfected state of primordial nature, which requires no perfecting. The Dzogchen practice is the most ancient and direct stream of wisdom within Tibet's Buddhist tradition to realize the true nature of mind. It is a clear, effective, and relevant practice for our turbulent times. There is an unbroken lineage of great realized Dzogchen masters from the ancient to present times.

Dzongsar Gompa: An important monastery in eastern Tibet in Derge.

Dzongsar Jamyang Khyentse Rinpoche: He is a reincarnate Tulku of Jamyang Khyentse Chökyi Lodrö. He was born in 1961 in eastern Bhutan and recognized as a reincarnate lama by Kyabjé Sakya Trizin. His root guru was Kyabjé Dilgo Khyentse Rinpoche and received empowerments and teachings from many greatest Tibetan masters including Kyabjé Sixteenth Karmapa, Kyabjé Dudjom Rinpoche, Kyabjé Sonam Zangpo Rinpoche, Kyabjé Chatral Rinpoche, Kyabjé Nyoshul Khen Rinpoche, Kyabjé Khenpo Appey, and many others. He is the founder of the Khyentse Foundation and 84000: Translating the Words of the Buddha. He has also written many Buddhist books in English: *What Makes You Not a Buddhist, Living is Dying, Not for Happiness*, and *Guru Drinks Bourbon?*

Generosity (Skt. dāna): It is a practice of cultivating giving to others; one of the most common examples is giving alms to poor and needy people.

Gompa: Monastery.

Guru Rinpoche (Guru Padmasambhava): A tantric master from Oddiyana who established Tantrayāna (Vajrayāna) Buddhism in Tibet and other Himalayan regions. Refer to Chapter 2 for more details.

***Konchog sum* (The Three Jewels)**: The Buddha, the Dharma, and the Sangha.

Kunchog Tso: My mother. She passed away in 2018 at the age of eighty-four.

Kyabjé: A Tibetan word used as an honorific title and show of respect for realized lamas. It means lord (*jé*) of refuge (*kyab*). Traditionally, a title to lamas of extraordinary realization and wisdom.

Longchen Nyingtik (Tib; Wyl. *klong chen snying thig*): It is one of the essence teachings in *Dzogpa Chenpo*. It was a mind *terma* revealed by Great Rigdzin Jigmé Lingpa (1730-1798) received directly from Guru Rinpoche and Gyalwa Longchen Rabjam. It is also the heart essence of the teachings of Dzogpa Chenpo. It is a complete path from the beginning to the enlightenment stage. One of the most widely practiced traditions.

Longchen Rabjam (Tib. *Klong chen rab 'byams*; Omniscient Longchenpa or Gyalwa Longchen Rabjam): He was one of the most brilliant spiritual masters and scholars in the Nyingmapa tradition. He systematized the Nyingmapa teachings, wrote extensively on Dzogchen, and transmitted the Longchen Nyingtik to Great Rigdzin Jigmé Lingpa. Out of his wisdom, Omniscient Longchenpa wrote more than 250 treatises covering all of Buddhist theory and practice up to Dzogchen. Many were lost during his return from Bhutan to Tibet. Those that survive are *The Seven Treasure*, *The Trilogy of Dispelling Darkness*, *The Trilogy of Finding Comfort and Ease*, *The Trilogy of Natural Freedom*, and other writings.

***Lung* (Tib; Wyl. *lung*; oral transmission)**: *Lung* is the oral transmission from a teacher to create an auspicious connection with the lineage of a particular text or practice. The oral transmission of tantric texts after one has received the associated empowerment.

Through the master, a student creates a link with the past masters and receives blessings from the lineage. The blessings help the student to understand the full depth of the text.

Mahāyāna (Skt.; Tib. *tekpa chenpo***; Wyl.** *theg pa chen po***)**: The great vehicle of the Bodhisattvas. The highest aspiration of Mahāyāna is to bring about the liberation of all sentient beings from sufferings to attain enlightenment.

Merit (Skt. Punya; Wyl. *bsod nams***)**: Merit is accumulating good karma through good deeds, thoughts, and actions of body, speech, and mind that contributes to growth in practice and that takes a person closer to the wisdom.

Mindroling Monastery: One of the six mother monasteries in Tibet in the Nyingmapa tradition. In 1676, it was founded by Minling Terchen Gyurme Dorje, aka Rigdzin Terdak Lingpa, and Lochen Dharmshri. After the passing of the eleventh throne holder Kyabjé Minling Terchen Rinpoche in 2008, the twelfth hereditary successor Dungse Dalha Gyaltsen Rinpoche from Tibet is the current throne holder.

Nāga (Skt. nāga; Tib. *lu***, Wyl.** *klu***)**: They are serpent spirits who live under the earth's surface, in water, trees, or rocks. They are associated with magical powers and great wealth. They are also responsible for some types of illnesses in humans.

Nālandā (Skt.): It was one of the largest and famous monastic universities in ancient India. Associated with great saints of Mahāyāna Buddhism, it was built during the Gupta Empire by Gupta King Kumaragupta I (415-455 CE). The Great Chinese master Hsüan-Tsang studied in this university for six years in the seventh century and later translated many valuable Buddhist texts into Chinese. At its peak, it was home to some ten thousand students who were only admitted after passing rigorous examinations and debates. Today it is a turned into a museum in the state of Bihar, India.

***Ngöndro* (Tib.)**: A preliminary practice in Vajrayāna Buddhism to help a path seeker or dweller develop unwavering faith and devotion to the Three Jewels. There are many types of such practices using their unique jargon and methods but with the same goal of achieving liberation. In the Nyingma school of Tibetan Buddhism, the preliminary practice is called *Ngöndro*. One such is the Longchen Nyingtik Ngöndro in Drogpa Chenpo. In this practice, one of the precious guides is the *"Words of My Perfect Teacher"* by Great Patrul Rinpoche, with a recent addition, *"Not for Happiness"* by Dzongsar Jamyang Khyentse Rinpoche—the former uses classic Buddhist examples while latter, more modern-day anecdotes of the 21st century. Another valuable resource book by Kyabjé Dodrupchen Rinpoche is the compilation of the step-by-step instructional manual of how to practice Ngöndro that includes aspirational prayers, mantras, visualization of deities, and meditation.[320] You can also read numerous commentaries by other great Tibetan masters.

Nirmānakāya: The physical manifestation body aspect of Buddhahood out of compassion to help sentient beings.

Nirvāna (Skt.): Liberation or enlightenment in English.

Nyingma or Nyingmapa: This is the oldest school of Tantrayāna Buddhism in Tibet. The principal founders of this school are Guru Padmasambhava, commonly known as Guru Rinpoche in Tibetan, the Nālandā abbot Śāntarakṣita, and Tibet's religious king Great Trisong Detsen. Together they established Buddhism in Tibet, the

---

[320] Lotsawa House, n.d., *The Excellent Path to Omniscience: The Dzogchen Preliminary Practice of Longchen Nyingtik*. Available for free download at https://www.lotsawahouse.org/tibetan-masters/dodrupchen-I/longchen-nyingtik.

Land of Snows, in the 8ᵗʰ century. They found the first monastic university of Samye, where Indian Buddhist scholars and Tibetan translators translated the Buddha Dharma from Sanskrit into Tibetan. Guru Rinpoche and Khandro Yeshé Tsogyal hid many *termas* for the benefit of future generations. These have become popular treasure teachings in Nyingmapa.

Pecha: In general, it is a generic name for Buddhist scriptures.

Phowa (Tib.; Wyl. *'pho ba*; Skt. utkrānti): This a powerful practice of directing the transference of consciousness at the time of death. It is either done by a practitioner for oneself at the moment of death, or by a master who does it for a deceased person. This practice is also included in Longchen Nyingtik.

Polu Khen Rinpoche: The root guru of my father. He was a highly learned Buddhist scholar and realized *Dzogpa Chenpo* meditator master. Polu Khen Rinpoche spent many years in India and spent the later years in Bhutan.

Prajna Paramita Sūtra (Skt. Prajñāpāramitāhṛdaya): This is one of the central teachings of Lord Buddha. The essence of this teaching is the concept of śūnyatā. Also known as The Heart Sūtra.

Punya (Skt.): See merit.

Rainbow body (Tib. *ja lü*; Wyl. *'ja' lus*): This is a phenomenon of enlightenment realized in *Dzogpa Chenpo*. A highly realized practitioner can transform his or her physical body into radiant light. There are many forms of the rainbow body: some will dissolve entirely into pure light, some will leave only the hair and nails behind, and others will have their bodies shrink to tiny sizes. This phenomenon is achieved through the practice of *trekchö* and *tögal*.

Rigdzin Jigmé Lingpa (1730-1798): He was one of the most important masters in the Nyingma lineage. He discovered the Longchen Nyingtik cycle of teachings and practice as mind *terma* through series of visions from Omniscient Longchenpa, blessings of Guru Rinpoche, and guidance of wisdom dākinīs. He is also known as Khyentse Özer because of his rays of compassion and wisdom.

Samadhi: Meditation.

Sambhogakāya: The luminous aspect of Buddhahood only noticeable to highly realized beings.

Sampa Lhundrupma: This is a prayer to Guru Rinpoche that spontaneously fulfills all wishes and removes all obstacles.

Samsāra (Skt.; Tib. *khowa*; Wyl. *'khor ba*): The continuous cyclic births and deaths characterized by sufferings, and one seeks to achieve liberation (nirvāna) from it.

Sangha: A community of all practitioners of the teachings of Buddha.

Śāriputra: One of the prominent disciples of Buddha Śākyamuni.

Śāstras (Skt.): The commentaries of the teachings of Buddha.

Seven-Line Prayer (Wyl. *tshig bdun gsol debs*): It is also known as The Seven Verses of the Vajra. The prayer is the invocation to Guru Rinpoche for his blessings. Refer to Chapter 3 for more details.

Śūnyatā (Skt.): Emptiness.

Sūtra (Skt.): The teachings spoken by the Buddha.

Sūtrayāna (Skt.; Tib. *dö tekpa*; Wyl. *mdo'i theg pa*): The teachings are designated as the "Causal Vehicle" for establishing the cause for attaining enlightenment.

Tantrika: A practitioner of Tantrayāna.

Tantrayāna Buddhism: The tantric form of Buddhism. There are many tantric Buddhist traditions followed in Asian countries. Also, see Vajrayāna.

Tārā (Skt.; Tib. *Drolma*; Wyl. *sgrol ma*): One of the most popular female enlightened deities closely associated with compassion and enlightened activity. She is the one who liberates sentient beings from the sufferings of samsāra. There are twenty-one manifestations of Tārā but the Green Tārā associated with protection and White Tārā associated with longevity are the most popular ones. There are complete paths of Tārā practices.

Tashi Phuntsok: My father. He passed away in 2017 at the age of ninety.

Tendrel (Tib.): The Tibetan word *tendrel* means "dependent arising" or "interdependence." Like *ten* means "to depend," and *drel* means "relationship," therefore, *tendrel* means that all phenomena come into existence through a dependent relationship with other phenomena. All situations arise through countless causes and conditions, karmic links.

Terma: Treasure teachings commonly found in Nyingmapa.

Tertön: A treasure revealer.

The Four Truths: The Four Truths are that all compounded things are impermanent, that all emotions are pain, that all things have no inherent existence, and that nirvāṇa is beyond conception.

Thuktam: It is when a person recognizes the luminosity and rests in meditation during the time of death. Refer to Chapter 4 for more details.

***Tsok* (Tib.; Wyl. *tshog; Skt.* ganacakra)**: A ritual in which a person offers Buddhist texts, Buddha statues, clothes, flowers, foods, drinks, and precious gems to Gurus or Buddhas or deities for their blessings. It is one of the most effective methods of accumulating merits, also one of the important practices in Vajrayāna.

Tulku: A reincarnate lama.

Vajrayāna: A Tantrayāna form of Buddhism practiced primarily in Tibet and some Himalayan regions of Bhutan, Nepal, eastern regions of India—now spreading across the globe. Also, there are practitioners of Tantrayāna in Japan, China, and South Korea.

Vimalakīrti: Great Mahayana Master. Refer to Chapter 5 for more details.

Vimalakīrti Nirdeśa Sūtra (Skt.; nirdeśa means "instructions, advice."): It is a Mahayana Buddhist sūtra commonly known as The Vimalakīrti Sūtra. Refer to Chapter 5 for more details.

Vipaśyanā (Skt.; Tib. *Lhakthong*): Profound insight of seeing the truth.

Wang (Tib.; Wyl. *dbang*; Skt. abhiseka): It means empowerment. It is a ritual through which a master empowers a disciple to follow a particular spiritual practice to recognize our true nature.

Yeshé Tsogyal: One of the most important Tibetan female masters. She was a dākinī (*Khandro*) in human form to benefit the sentient beings, particularly the people of Tibet, lovingly known as Khandro Yeshé Tsogyal. She was one of the twenty-five disciples of Guru Rinpoche and one of the most influential and instrumental in concealing many treasure teachings (*terma*) of Guru Rinpoche for the benefit of the future generations. Khandro Yeshé Tsogyal was like the warm rays of the radiating sun of Guru Rinpoche and propagated Buddhism extensively across the entire Himalayan regions. Refer to Chapter 4 for more details.

Yeshu: Tibetan word for Christian.

Zhitro (Tib. *shyitro*; Wyl. *zhi khro*): It literally means the peaceful (*zhi*) and wrathful (*tro*) deities. Usually, *Zhitro* refers to the Hundred Peaceful and Wrathful Deities (Tib. *shitro rik gya*; Wyl. *zhi khro rigs brgya*).

Appendix A

The Seven-Line Prayer in Tibetan

ༀ༔ །གུ་རུ་རིན་པོ་ཆེའི་ཚིག་བདུན་གསོལ་འདེབས་བཞུགས་སོ། །

ཧཱུྃ༔ ཨོ་རྒྱན་ཡུལ་གྱི་ནུབ་བྱང་མཚམས༔
hung orgyen yul gyi nubjang tsam

པདྨ་གེ་སར་སྡོང་པོ་ལ༔
pema gesar dongpo la

ཡ་མཚན་མཆོག་གི་དངོས་གྲུབ་བརྙེས༔
yatsen chok gi ngödrub nyé

པདྨ་འབྱུང་གནས་ཞེས་སུ་གྲགས༔
pema jungné shyé su drak

འཁོར་དུ་མཁའ་འགྲོ་མང་པོས་བསྐོར༔
khor du khandro mangpö kor

ཁྱེད་ཀྱི་རྗེས་སུ་བདག་བསྒྲུབ་ཀྱི༔
khyé kyi jesu dak drub kyi

བྱིན་གྱིས་བརླབ་ཕྱིར་གཤེགས་སུ་གསོལ༔
jingyi lab chir shek su sol

གུ་རུ་པདྨ་སིདྡྷི་ཧཱུྃ༔
guru pema siddhi hung

Appendix B

The Eight Manifestations of Guru Rinpoche[321]

The Eight Manifestations of Guru Rinpoche (Tib. *guru tsen gyé*) are the eight principal forms assumed by Guru Rinpoche at different points in his life:

1. Guru Tsokyé Dorje: Lake-born Vajra (birth)
2. Guru Shakya Sengé: Lion of the Shakyas (ordination)
3. Guru Nyima Özer: Rays of the Sun (subjugating demonic spirits)
4. Guru Padmasambhava: Lotus-born (establishing Buddhism in Tibet)
5. Guru Loden Choksé: Wise Seeker of the Sublime (mastery of the teachings)
6. Guru Pema Gyalpo: The Lotus King (kingship)
7. Guru Sengé Dradrok: The Lion's Roar (subjugation of non-Buddhists)
8. Guru Dorje Drolö: Wild Wrathful Vajra (concealing terma, binding spirits under oath)

---

[321] Rigpa Shedra, 2017.

The Eight Manifestations reflect the ability to appear in different forms for different needs and demands of the sentient beings. In Tibetan, they are called as "the eight names of the Guru (Tib. *guru tsen gye*)," depicting different manifestations of the innermost nature of mind.

Appendix C

Motivation and Success
by David Gration

It is good when young people want to work hard at the start of their career and earn enough to be independent from and also support their parents. However, if they exaggerate the importance of money above all else in their lives, and overlook the real potential motivation in their work, they may enter a trap from which they don't escape all through a busy, even workaholic, financially dominated career.

In the Second Distraction, Tashi Gelek has expressed his thoughts at the start of his career but he later considered what motivation really meant for him. Now he thinks differently, but not necessarily exactly as this appendix, and this Distraction no longer blocks his way to the Buddhist Path.

Before settling into a life of seeing money as the only thing that matters, consider this, which might help clarify our thoughts on our true motivation and find deeper criteria for what success means to us:

There are two factors: The motivation **within-the-job** itself, in the work we do, and what comes to us from outside the job, **from the environment** within which we do the work.

Let us explore our work motivation through these two factors.

Within the job are powerful motivators which drive us, through our most important work needs, for achievement, with some excitement perhaps, to give of our very best. Your job is not a prison. It is your duty to yourself and your family, but it can also be your friend. If anybody can reshape the work, it is you.

The environment factors can demotivate if they are unsatisfactory, but however important and generous the pension scheme is, it will never motivate us above a habitual level of working.

What follows is what I learned from many successful decades in the top and senior managerial jobs in international business and from hundreds of intelligent managers interpreting their experience and success. Also, from my academic career of learning, teaching and researching management and motivation, and from other academics' research and writing.

Here are what have settled down, in a science-based model, to be the main sets of in-job needs. Each of the five sets is followed by some practical ways, amenable to Buddhist practice, to achieve success through these needs:

Interesting work with positive sense of purpose and clarity of expectations

If you are a manager, discuss with your staff individually and as a team the purpose of each job, their main areas of responsibility (not detailed tasks) which determine success, their authority (how far they can go without asking you), and reasonable standards for each responsibility given their levels of authority.

You could ask your manager for a similar discussion about your job, and it might be best to start there.

The idea is not only to clarify the job, but to find along the way more interesting ways to do the job and more inspiring was of looking at purposes.

It is not a matter of agreeing and signing a formal job description for the files of the Human Resources Department. Aim to reach an informal and flexible shared understanding which then evolves with job changes.

This takes a little well spent time but saves more and usually people are pleasantly surprised by the results and like their jobs more. The job should now be a base for a Buddhist path in and outside work, and a base for the rest of these sets of needs.

Targets for improvements, variety of new and creative projects, sense of direction, challenge

Instead of telling your staff what their targets are, discuss with them What Result could be achieved and How Much of it, by When. Get their ideas and emphasize their freedom to choose How to achieve the target with methods from their experience and creativity, Generally people want to do a good job and good management avoids preventing them from doing so.

If targets are agreed and seen to be realistic if we push ourselves somewhat, they are more likely to be achieved. If a target is imposed and seems impossible, it is a self-fulfilling prophecy with its excuses for failure built in ready. There is no point in dreaming up results which won't be achieved. Honesty is better, and confidence.

This process also takes time but with a fast return on the investment through a reduced need to supervise and the avoidance of duplication of effort and crossed purposes.

More targets should be agreed with the team which also takes less time than with each individual separately. Divide and rule does not fit with Buddhism.

Responsibility, freedom from supervision, discovery through new projects

DELEGATE! for less pressure and more time, removing another obstacle to managers' practicing Buddhism.

Easy to say, but possible to do if we think it through with a framework which can make barriers disappear, for example:

- There are two forms of delegation: Try both, already introduced them in the two paragraphs above. There is delegation of one-off projects, with targets and trust, and the other is continuing delegation of more responsibility and authority through overall job clarification and enrichment.
- Agree to review points to avoid constant supervision.
- Managers should make it clear to junior managers that the ability to delegate well is compulsory for promotion. No

overworked harrassed "quicker to do it myself" supervisor can be considered for management.

- Working late at the office should be explained as preventing promotion to a job with greater organizing requirements. Crawling and politics should also be seen to stop promotion.

A good manager sees no need to work longer hours than staff.

There is no point trying to explain why you can't delegate more. Your manager knows all the excuses, and you would only be digging yourself deeper into the hole.

Managers often have a delegation barrier which is not knowing you want bigger things delegated. Tell them.

Learning and growth for achievement

Training in new and stronger skills should not be confined to training center classrooms or luxurious hotels. Coaching in the job is the manager's responsibility and opportunity. Invest time rather than money.

The better trained your staff are, the more time you have. Learn more about Buddhism and use the time to practice.

Training is for the present and changing job, and for an imminent next job.

Development is for further ahead and jobs not yet identified.

Lifelong learning. See Information Panel #6 Japanese Management for lifelong learning and lifelong everything.

One of the best methods of training and development is the appraisal discussion, which also helps identify training needs and development opportunities as well as evaluating the success of training:

Recognition

Not only for results achieved but also for how they were achieved. Appraisal is not a bookkeeping exercise. Teamwork, skills successfully applied, ideas shared, others' ideas encouraged and applied, all aspects of contributions to teams.

Appraisal is more than mere assessment, one way and top-down. Appraisal is a discussion which starts with self-appraisal, and is mutual: the manager's contribution is also reviewed.

Appraisal is not an inquest on the past but planning the future, work changes, training, and development. What will be done differently, and new projects. Show up to meetings more often and on time, better prepared. The manager will listen more carefully and communicate more face-to-face, not always by email.

Appraisal with the team, the manager should not be afraid.

Appraisal is not the time to discuss salary: that is a separate time and different occasion.

Focus on your job, using the above model if you find this helpful. Review what you do and where you could do things differently, bringing more real motivation, and more conducive to Buddhism— with new advantages in time and spirituality for Path-seeking. Reconsider the Money and Success Distraction. Discuss this with your colleagues.

Discuss with your manager: not by complaints but through questions, and make suggestions. If the manager is not interested in motivation, select a better manager (in business, you have plenty to choose from) with a little organizational shift of your work or a new job. If the whole company is resistant, consider a move to a better company—or to a more compassionate industry (they are not all the same). This will be difficult if you are in Japanese lifetime employment (see Information Panel #6).

To complete the full model, **The Environment Factors** in which we do the job, de-motivating if unsatisfactory but never motivating up to top performance, is, therefore, less important then from in-job motivation. It can be seen from three angles than the 4th and biggest:

The **Physical Environment**, working conditions. Our work probably suffers when we are too cold, and when we are warm enough, we are no longer de-motivated but temperature can't cause positive higher motivation. Business Class might make flying less de-motivating and we are more rested on arrival but that's all.

The **Security Environment** around our job, terms of employment. If we are constantly afraid of dismissal for mysterious sudden reasons, that's de-motivating. The way some companies deliberately play on this, destroying confidence, trust, and productivity, is inexplicable. But job security does not deliver top performance and nor does membership of a good superannuation scheme, important though this is.

Our **Social Environment** at work: if colleagues are hostile and you feel an outcast, this is miserable. But a kind, friendly bunch can't love us to high motivation if the work we do is simply not motivating.

Teamwork is vital but needs the context of all the in-job motivators to succeed. And we don't have to turn up to all the barbecues and the company dinner dance if we don't want to.

Now to the more controversial **Financial Environment** in which we work, where the same points apply. If company Compensation Management was not paying enough to feed the family and meet the mortgage repayments that would be really de-motivating. So we work hard, get promoted, bring home a decent wage. When we are paid enough—and some more for a nice life—the motivational benefits of extra money start to wear off, and it becomes more a status thing than a need. How much is enough? Another new car, already? does not get the very best from us, and did we need to get to such a big mortgage?

Too-low pay de-motivates. Too-high pay does not motivate, and not if we feel we aren't earning it or we don't like the job anyway.

Pay a generous salary, increasing steadily over the years, according to the job and how the employee does it, and the team. Bonus pay in bits and pieces don't lead to top performance and self-fulfillment (nor self-esteem, self-actualization, and other jargon). The play on greed is counter-productive for motivation. Individual bonuses cause negative competition and damage teamwork. The criteria rarely make practical sense, so we are motivated to take the bonus but not to do the job well in the way we know it should be done. We feel miserable and under pressure, at work and outside.

Money gets us to work but not to work well while we are there. Our motivation can't be bought; we are more difficult to bribe than inexperienced managers imagine.

Pay might get us to work more, harder, but not better.

Consider your work-life balance, through all the factors in this paper. You will probably find amongst the in-job needs the greatest gains for true motivation, the success of the employing organization, and the time and mental, spiritual space (emptiness?) to find the Path, free from the Second Distraction.

We don't have to see success in terms of how much they pay us. There are better measures now we know where to look for them.

When I was putting all this into practice, I had not been introduced to Buddhism. Now I am seeing it in terms of **Samsāra** and **Śūnyatā**.

Samsāra is in the environment factors, familiar, safe, easy, no change, don't have to think hard.

The in-job motivation is Śūnyatā, adventurous, perhaps a little risky but with high potential returns if we step outside our comfortable habits.

Japanese Managemenet
by David Gration

The Buddhist foundation for Japanese management "style" and behaviour in organizations not only guides and strengthens management but also enables the path-seeker to secure more time and overcome obstacles to practice Buddhism—which is the aim of this book.

Traditional management practices from Japan's history as a homogeneous society with a culture of shared thinking are still broadly applied in today's modern commercial environment, since the third century when Confucian compassion entered Japanese culture and later broadened through the four truths of Buddhism.

During my international business career, I worked for and with Japanese companies and managers and witnessed and admired how Japanese management fits with religion and Japanese culture. In my academic career, I learned from Japanese students and teachers, and through my research, about generosity, humility, patience, how the self does not exist independently, and—especially from Tashi Gelek in recent years—how managers can be less aggressive and more effective.

Here are the Japanese management practices which have stayed with me most impressively:

Consensus decision process

This takes time, to build the commitment to the better decisions which result from consensus, and to defuse potential resistance and power struggles. But it saves more time because consensus decisions are implemented faster and more effectively.

These decisions succeed because more and better ideas and experiences have been considered, and different interests are taken into account. This wider consultation does not closely reflect the hierarchy and the outcome is not mere obedience to on high.

The decisions are debated with those who have something of value to contribute, those who will have to implement, and others who will be affected.

The time available is increased by taking fewer but bigger radical decisions with significant changes of direction, rather than too many little decisions separately. Japanese managers are amused by western colleagues taking so many decisions so fast—because they keep getting them wrong, so have to take more "repair" decisions.

Japanese consensus decisions are not the same as western more formal "participative management," with committees, and less natural. Japanese workgroups are expected to take their own decisions about how to get the job done and improve results, and employees are encouraged to implement their own creative, experienced and responsible choices.

This is not the same as a Suggestion Scheme offering ideas to higher management to accept, reject or ignore, possibly with a little "perk" payment as if creativity can be bought.

Buddhist patience and generosity.

Teamworking and group working

Organizational harmony in a holistic society goes with a collective rather than individualistic culture.

Individuals are not singled out for their performance, which can't be distinguished from that of the whole team.

Employees impress by helping and cooperating with colleagues and taking pride in the team's achievements, not by displaying their own brilliance and taking personal credit.

Even a manager who wanted to be authoritarian could not be because of the power of team cohesion.

Buddhist modesty, humility, and generosity.

We have looked at team decisions, team motivation, and job clarification in Information Panel #4, and there is also team pay and team training, But most of all day-to-day team working.

The whole motivational approach in Information Panel #4 was easier for me to apply to Japan than in any other country.

Secure employment

Reinforcing corporate social responsibility, Belonging to your organisation more than to your specialism or profession means that you are not a production engineer but a Toyota production engineer. Or just "I work for Honda." You are a generalist more than a specialist and the company is a stronger family than professional links across other companies and organizations.

Sony looks after your welfare, not the Mechanical Engineers Association. Company Unions rather than specialist Trade Unions.

Security is naturally part of the agreement, rather than constant threat and uncertainty.

Careers move through a series of jobs and perhaps specialisms, but broad line experience is most important in lasting career planning.

Training does not cease for older employees with the emphasis moving to prevention of decline: developing new skills continues, to improve further and adjust to change. Similarly, for younger and all employees, when a certain level of competence has been reached training is not finished, and continues for further advance and other jobs.

The simplified "Lifetime Employment" can't be available to everybody. For the company to adjust to demand fluctuations some employees have to be temporary, and women used to be confined to this category. I hope by now there has been progress towards equal security.

There is also lifetime learning and lifetime development, which was also not for everybody.

Buddhist diligence and discipline.

Seniority

Steadily upward careers are geared to length of service, with less of the competitive seeking for rapid personal promotions which can disrupt organizational security.

Orderly career advance is based less on numerical results and more on how they have been achieved, whether the transferable skills most useful higher up are demonstrated, how you work with and contribute to the team effort and consensus, how you are coming along from specialisms to generalist.

Buddhist patience and humility.

Seniority is not only for promotion but also for pay—with benefits—(and in return for long-term loyalty) rather than the individualistic scramble for advantage over colleagues.

In separating this note into different aspects of Japanese management, we see the same principles recurring, and we must retain the holistic view of Japanese management. That is the point: all this holds together, each aspect reinforcing the others. That is why a complete management system which has grown in one complete culture can't be transplanted into a totally different complete culture. Japanese management can't work in the USA or England, and attempts to impose preferred bits from it have proved disastrous.

However, Buddhist practice thrives in different cultures, being spiritual whereas management is more practical and mundane, more subject to technological and cultural compatibility.

Tashi Gelek's description of Shikoku Henro reflects on how an ancient pilgrimage has lived on for over a thousand years and continues in today's modern commercial society. The cultural fundamentals, however, have remained the same and that continuity of values also explains the survival of the Japanese management style. Since my retirement, the management environment has changed, so many details of management in action must have altered. But as Tashi Gelek and I see it the above basics remain.

Index

Lightning Source UK Ltd.
Milton Keynes UK
UKHW010901100921
390347UK00002B/258